TREE OF HOPE

TREE OF
HOPE

Anne Frank's Father Shares His Wisdom With An American Teen and the World

CARA WILSON-GRANAT

(REVISED EDITION)

Charleston, SC
www.PalmettoPublishing.com

Tree of Hope
Copyright © 2021 by Cara Wilson Granat

First Edition

Paperback ISBN: 978-1-63837-123-6
Hardcover ISBN: 978-1-63837-124-3
eBook ISBN: 978-1-63837-125-0

In honor of Otto Frank, my eternal Tree of Hope

Table of Contents

Forward		ix
Preface		xi
Introduction		xv
Chapter 1	Back to the Beginning	1
Chapter 2	A Teenager in the Sixties	6
Chapter 3	Love and Marriage	18
Chapter 4	Political and Social Awakening	28
Chapter 5	A New Life	41
Chapter 6	A Visit Missed, A Visit Planned	61
Chapter 7	A Dream Realized	72
Chapter 8	Otto: Infinite Signs	85
Chapter 9	Epilogue: Changes	103
Chapter 10	Shared Lessons from Otto	110
Appendix		143

Forward

Otto Frank became a friend who validated my thoughts and feelings. Ultimately, even my words. He was the father of Anne Frank, who wrote *The Diary of Anne Frank* and mentor of hope to a global family of children who sought out his guidance and love. How he was able to give each of us so much attention and hope when most of us had neither at key times in our lives, I will never know. I was but one of "Otto's Children," yet he always made me feel important. How grateful I will always be for the gift of such friendship.

In this latest and final revised edition—the fourth of a series of different publications through the years about my longtime correspondence and friendship with Otto Frank--I've featured some key letters, photographs, and the shared lessons I learned from my wise Tree of Hope mentor. I hope they offer comfort to all as well.

I am so grateful to my beloved family and friends far too many to list, some blessedly still here and some long past, including dear Buddy Elias, who wrote such supportive words for me before he died a few years ago. He and his lovely wife, Gerti (Bambi) were always so encouraging of me and my desire to keep our wonderful Otto and Anne alive in every way. My beautiful parents, long gone, Aaron and Lilly Weiss, were always there with such support throughout[1] this long-life passage; Kent Wilson who encouraged me to finally meet my darling Otto in person at last. I will always be grateful that he made that transformative journey possible and so timely; and my wonderful sons, who have grown up with "Uncle Otto and Aunt Fritzi"—familiar, far-away fixtures throughout their lives (gifting them with delicious ginger cookies every year), Ethan and Jesse Wilson—my "trees of hope," who, along with Fabiane and Branda, continue to give me infinite hope along with the next generation of "trees"--their beautiful sons, my cherished grandsons, Kaio and Nicholas.

Special thanks to dearest Adam and Faina Granat for continually cheering me on; deep and enduring love to my "Otto's Children" beloved soul brothers, Father John Neiman and Ryan Cooper who are always there with such love and shared wisdom; to the splendid Nathan Weissler who inspires me with his courage and passionate vision; wonderful Federica Pannocchia (Founder/President of Un Ponte per Anne Frank), Barbara Eldridge (Anne Frank Fonds), and Vince Pankoke Jr. (Lead Case Agent, Cold Case Diary) for their continuous encouragement and loving support; to Shawn Cauthen (Director, "Call Me Papa"); Michael Burns, (TEDx Coach Extraordinaire) and his phenomenal team, including glorious Marian Houser; Tim Whittome and Joop van Wijk-Voskuijl ("Meeting" Anne Frank, An Anthology); many kudos to Palmetto Publishing especially Roy Francia, Kristin Graham, and the entire staff for their patience, compassion and vision helping me birth this final Otto Frank legacy so beautifully. Finally, special eternal gratitude and love to my Rock, Peter Granat, my perpetual "Peach," for steadying the course with the infinite gifts he is in my life. Blessings to all.

Photo Credits:
Cara Wilson-Granat
Father John Neiman
Ryan Cooper
Buddy Elias

Preface

No other words could better define Otto than his worldwide, loving correspondence with young people. How can one understand the greatness of a human being who suffered the hell of Auschwitz, whose children, wife and friends were murdered by the most inhuman criminal regime of our time, and whose philosophy remained: "In spite of everything, I still believe that people are really good at heart." These words were written by his daughter in the world-famous *The Diary of Anne Frank*.

As she grew up, Anne undoubtedly was inspired by her father's character, and this integrity did not diminish even after his family's hiding place was betrayed and his family murdered. In 1946, one year after the war ended, he traveled to Germany to visit the people he had known before his capture, to make sure they never sided with the betrayer, whose name he knew. Otto held no hate, nor any feelings of revenge. To the many people who asked him to reveal the name of the traitor, he refused, saying: "It will injure the children of the man, knowing their father is in jail." The suspect nevertheless did have to answer in court, but was not sentenced since his guilt could not be proven.

Naturally, Otto was never able to forget the loss of his family, and often the remembrance of his beloved ones led to tears and depression. But then he saw the worldwide impact of his daughter's diary and decided to dedicate the rest of his life to its humanistic messages. Within a relatively short time, *The Diary of Anne Frank* became an international bestseller and was adapted for stage and screen, continuing to influence generation after generation. It remains a timeless and unique plea against discrimination, racial hatred and anti-Semitism.

Otto co-founded the Anne Frank Fonds in Amsterdam and the Anne-Frank-Fonds in Basel, Switzerland. He was received by royalty, Pope John XXIII, and the heads of governments, always accepting the many honors bestowed on him in Anne's name. His deepest wish, as was his daughter's was the longing for unification of mankind and peace on earth, especially among the different religions. A Japanese church, named the Anne Frank Rose Church, warmed his heart, as well as peace projects between the Israelis and Arabs.

It was a great blessing that Otto met Fritzi Geiringer, who became his wife in 1953. Her husband and son had also perished in the concentration camps, and together they dedicated the rest of their lives to spreading the healing words of Anne's diary. They lived in our home for 7 years before moving to their own modest apartment in a suburb of Basel, Switzerland.

Over the years, thousands of letters were written to Otto, mostly by young girls moved by Anne's life and words; many of them asked him for advice about their own problems. Many adults also felt the need to write and express their admiration and sympathy for him; he answered every letter personally, usually responding just one time to the enormous volume of mail from around the world.

But with Cara, it was different. They developed, over time, a deep friendship, and through their exchange of thoughts and feelings, the relationship deepened into a profound grandfather-daughter love, which sustained each of them. After Otto's death, the love with Cara continued with my wife Gerti and me.

For all of us, Otto remains unforgettable. He was a tower of strength in spite of his sorrow. What impressed me most was his young mind and understanding of the problems of each generation. Children and youngsters loved him, accepted his advice, and turned to him with all their worries and sorrows; in return, he offered them hope and understanding. Otto was a mensch: the best we can say about a human being.

Cara was one of those marvelous, sensitive youngsters who gave him so much love, and was loved by him in return. She honored him with this book…and he deserves it. Thank you, Cara, for you, too, are a blessing in this troubled world!

Buddy Elias, Cousin of Anne Frank
President of the Anne Frank-Fonds in Basel, Switzerland

Introduction

On June 12, 1942, a young Jewish teenager living in Amsterdam, Holland, was given a little red-checked diary on her thirteenth birthday. One month later, she and her family—father, mother, and older sister—were forced to flee into hiding. Under Hitler's terrorist regime, all Jews and others not deemed pure Aryan were chosen to be ethnically "cleansed:" trapped and killed like cattle. Six million were annihilated in horrific concentration camps.

In hopes of saving his little family, Otto Frank, an esteemed and well-to-do German businessman, moved his wife, Edith, and daughters, Margot and Anne, from Germany to Amsterdam into a housing project, then into a secret annex above his spice factory.

The hiding place had several very small rooms, and a larger space with a sink, stove and storage two floors above the factory workers below, who knew nothing of it. It was one level above the four office workers who kept the secret. Miep Gies, Otto Frank's secretary and close personal friend of the family, became their lifeline, bringing them food, clothing, books, and news daily.

From early in the morning until way after dark after the last factory worker shut the door, the hidden Jews, which now included the Frank family, the Van Pels family, including son Peter, (Van Daan in the diary) and a dentist, Fritz Pfeffer (Albert Dussel) were forced into silence. Pattering around the floor on stocking feet, they were not allowed to make any sound which might give away their presence: no voices above a whisper, no laughing, coughing, using water, flushing the toilet, or any sounds that could possibly alert anyone to their existence. At night, after everyone had left, they could go down to the office and talk and move around unseen because the windows were blackened by dark curtains; still they had to move with utmost caution so the neighbors would not detect anything unusual.

During those endless days, weeks, months—ultimately two years—Anne Frank, the younger daughter, would write her thoughts and feelings in that little diary and on any papers and notebooks Miep could smuggle up to her. The young girl wrote about her deepest fears and joys, perceptions of her limited world, and her hopes and passionate desires. Everything about her was alive, alert and sensitive.

It truly seemed as if they would survive. The war was almost over; Hitler's Nazi armies were slowly being pushed back by the American and Russian troops and those left alive in the concentration camps would eventually be freed. But it was not to be: someone betrayed them…someone discovered the hiding place and turned them in.

On August 4, 1944, five men entered the office building. One of them wore the uniform of the German police. The others wore civilian clothes—probably Dutch Nazis. The men knew exactly where the doorway was hidden behind a bookshelf. They got the office workers to unlock the secret door and entered the apartment, gathered the terrified people, and began herding them down the stairs and into a large van parked out front. Miep never got to say goodbye to her friends. She only remembers the hollow sound of their feet coming down the stairs behind her.

Miep was told that when one of the men had turned over a footlocker and discovered Otto Frank's highly respected World War I German officer's uniform, the Nazi almost saluted him. "Take your time, take your time," he said, but then dragged him away with the others.

Once they left, Miep, her husband Jan (Henk in the diary), Bep (Elli), and Van Maaren (Van Motto), the warehouseman, went upstairs and witnessed the destruction the Nazis had left in their wake. In their haste to gather valuables, jewels and money, they left the most valuable gift of all: what was to become *The Diary of Anne Frank*. Scattered all over the floor were masses of papers and the little red-checked diary, all written by Anne.

Respecting the teenager's privacy, Miep quickly retrieved all the papers and placed them in her desk until the time when Anne would return from the concentration camp. Fortunately for the world, Miep never read any of it. Had she done so, she tells us now, she would have destroyed the papers because she and her husband and others would have been killed. It was a crime punishable by death to aid Jews in hiding or to have any Jewish possessions, so she kept the writings hidden in her desk, totally unaware of their value to the world. How could anyone have guessed the penning of a young girl would become one of our enduring literary treasures?

On January 27, 1945, Otto Frank was freed from Auschwitz after it was liberated by the Russian army. He started the painfully slow journey back to this home in Amsterdam on March 5, 1945. He and another group of survivors were accompanied by the Russians to the port of Odessa on the Black Sea; from there, he went by boat to Marseilles in France, and continued by train and truck to Holland. He arrived in Amsterdam on June 3, and immediately sought his friends, Miep and Jan Gies. Almost two months later, while he worked in his old office, Otto received word that Anne and Margot would never be coming home. His daughters had perished just a few weeks before liberation; Otto knew only that his wife had died in Auschwitz before the girls. Of all those hidden in the attic only Otto survived.

Broken and numb by the enormity of this final, insurmountable loss, Otto closed the door to his office asking not to be disturbed. Only then did Miep open her desk and remove Anne's writings and placed them in front of the grieving father.

"Here..." she said, "...is your daughter's legacy."

By the time I was picked to audition for the Twentieth Century Fox movie, "*The Diary of Anne Frank*," Anne's diary was world-famous.

It was the mid-fifties, I was twelve years old and had just barely discovered who Anne Frank was. But I knew one thing. Anne spoke to my heart as Otto Frank had listened to hers. Moved to the depths of my soul, I needed to talk to this wonderful man. And so I did for many, many years...

CHAPTER 1

Back to the Beginning

The movement of the train was hypnotic. Swaying back and forth, I felt my thoughts lulled into a comfortable twilight zone, back to the past where this strange pilgrimage had first started. Clickety-clickety…lush woods, pastures, quaint cottages, and reed-fringed lakes appeared and vanished as if in a dream. Blink. A gabled roof. Blink. Windswept bridges. Blink. Windmills! This wasn't a dream… this was the outskirts of Amsterdam. And I was on this train at last— me, Cara, a young mother of two little boys—alone for the first time in my life.

My husband, Kent, and sons, Ethan, age seven and Jesse age five, were far away in the United States. Kent had encouraged me to do this ever since he'd gone on a business trip to Amsterdam and visited the Anne Frank House. I'd pictured this happening since I was twelve years old. That's when I first discovered Anne Frank and the wonderful man I grew to love as my own grandfather—Anne's father, Otto.

It was 1977, and here I was, sitting on two huge parcels of luggage, because they were too heavy to drag any further. The train was jammed full with travelers, and I was sweltering from trying to shove my tons of stuff into the third car far away. I found a corner and collapsed from exhaustion and the stifling heat. Then the reality hit big-time: my dream was coming true.

It had begun happening very fast just weeks before, with a call I placed from the United States to Otto Frank in Basel, Switzerland, where he had lived for many years.

"Hello, Otto? Is it really you?"

"Cara, Cara! Is this you, Cara?"

His voice, like mine, was filled with emotion. We were speaking for the first time after eighteen years of correspondence.

"Yes, Otto—it's true! If you and Fritzi will be home the last week of July, I'll visit you."

"Cara, I am too nervous to talk further. Here, you must tell Fritzi of these things. We want very much to see you!"

The plan was for me to fly to Amsterdam, where I'd visit the Anne Frank House in the company of Miep Gies, Otto's Frank's faithful employee who had sheltered the family from the Nazis and saved Anne's diary, unread, for Otto. And then I would travel by train to Basel to meet Otto himself, my beloved friend and correspondent, along with his dear Fritzi, his second wife, whom he had met coming back from the camps after both of their families had been murdered. It was her daughter, Eva, who had been a playmate of Anne's and recognized her father, Otto Frank, and introduced him to her mother.

That call was a beginning to a fulfillment of a dream that had begun to take shape when, at age twelve, growing up in Southern California's San Fernando Valley, I had been chosen by a talent scout for the Twentieth Century-Fox film studio to audition for the starring role in the movie *The Diary of Anne Frank*.

I didn't get the part, but by now I had found a whole new world. Anne Frank's diary, which I read and reread, spoke to me about my dilemmas, anxieties and secret passions. She had felt the way I did. Yet she didn't tell anybody but her diary. In her cramped, secret world of hiding, Anne Frank hid her thoughts, too.

It was 1957, the year that Martin Luther King Jr. formed a group called the Montgomery Improvement Association, which organized a bus boycott in Montgomery, Alabama, which forced a bus company to desegregate. I remember being intensely interested that there was a world outside my comfortable little valley-girl existence. It was a cruel one, very different from my own, and I knew I needed to know more. But I was too involved in being me.

In those days, I was listening to love songs on the radio: Pat Boone crooning "April Love" and "Love Letters in the Sand," and Tab Hunter singing "Young Love." How I wanted to be in love like that! I watched movies: Bus Stop, Carousel, and my favorite, Bridge on the River Kwai. Like other girls, I teased and sprayed my hair into one of those loathsome beehive hairdos and dressed shapeless "sack" dresses, while the guys slicked their hair into "cool" ducktails. How I hated those days! I never seemed to look as pretty as the "soshes", the "in girls" who had jock stars for boyfriends, and had acne-free faces and far more womanly shapes than my flatness. I would look in the mirror and cry. Nothing worked, and I was miserable being Cara.

When I discovered Anne Frank, I was on the brink of the awful abyss of teenagedom and I, too, needed someone to confide in.

My parents were loving supports in my life, but I idealized the intense relationship Anne had with her father. (Ironically, Anne, too, expressed a longing for more attention from her father.) My own father was actively involved in the administration side of running a synagogue; Dad's whole life was a series of meetings. At home, he was too tired or unhappy to unload upon.

I had something else in common with Anne. We both had to share with sisters who were prettier and smarter than we felt we were.

As a young Jewish girl, I identified so strongly with this eloquent girl of my own age, that I believe I became her in my own mind. Her predicament burned in my thoughts: How she stayed in that tiny annex above her father's spice factory in Holland, cramped and bursting with frustrated life, "like a canary in a cage." How had she endured being hidden for two years in that claustrophobic space with her parents, Otto and Edith, her older sister, Margot, and another family the Van Daans, and their son, Peter, and the dentist, Mr. Dussel? After all she had been through, how could she still believe that "people are really good at heart?" She wrote, "If I look up to the heavens, I think that it will all come right, and that peace and tranquility will return again." She gave me hope.

Despite the monumental differences in our situations, to this day I feel that Anne helped me get through the teens with a sense of inner focus. She spoke for me. She was strong for me. She had so much trust in the future when I was ready to call it quits. I have since realized that so many young people feel very similarly about Anne Frank—a sense of kindred-spiritness. She speaks our language—a language of the heart and longing.

After my audition, I was able to get Otto's address in Basel from the office of George Stevens, director of the movie *The Diary of Anne Frank*. But would Mr. Frank answer me? Did he speak English? Could I even talk to him of Anne, or would it be too painful? I wrote and waited.

Then on a hot summer day just a few weeks before dreaded school resumed, an airmail letter from Switzerland was delivered. I must have reread it a hundred times! Somehow it made little difference that he wanted no part of an ongoing correspondence.

August 21, 1959

Dear Cara,

I received your kind letter and thank you for it. It was very nice of you to send me your photo, so that I have a better impression of your person...Anne's ardent wish was to work for mankind and therefore an Anne Frank Foundation has been incorporated in Amsterdam to work in her spirit. In the house in which we have been hiding, an International Youth Center will be established and maybe you will be able to visit it and work for it when your plan to come to Europe one day can be realized. You are right that I receive many letters from young people all over the world, but you will understand that it is not possible for me to carry on correspondence, though, as you see, I am answering to everyone.

Wishing you all the best, I am with kindest regards,

Yours,

Otto Frank

I remember answering that he was not to worry, he didn't have to answer me. I would simply write to him whether he answered me or not. Well, what choice did the poor man have? Whenever an attack of "I-can't-take-this-any-longer" would hit me, I'd put it all into lengthy letters to my distant friend, Otto Frank. It must have all been too intense to ignore, for he would always answer me. Thus, as they say in the movies, began our long friendship. As the traumas of my life arose, he never scoffed nor condescended to my teenage angst, but gave me his sincere opinion.

CHAPTER 2
A Teenager in the Sixties

My country was heading into one of the most devastating, passionate decades in its history: the Sixties. It was marked by peace marches, sometimes-violent protests against the war in Vietnam, and race riots. Everything seemed to be point-counterpoint: Congress passed the Civil Rights Act of 1960, which addressed voter registration practices. It didn't allow for enforcement of the act, however, so it was essentially ineffective.

And, in contrast to Martin Luther King's Southern Christian Leadership Conference (SCLS), dedicated to non-violent protest to draw attention to discrimination, another group was born. This was the Student Nonviolent Coordinating committee (SNCC), formed during a lunch counter sit-in in Greensboro, North Carolina. Though it called itself nonviolent, in truth it advocated direct, militant action: the iron fist inside the glove.

Even though I remember being aware of these issues bubbling to the surface in the papers and on TV, the arrogance of my youth was apparent. It took many more years before my letters reflect the pain of the times I was living in. Either I didn't want to face it, or it simply didn't affect me. I was a white teenager, full of hopes and dreams that seemed to have reason to come true.

I lived in a comfortable cocoon. The times had an insidious innocence, and I was part of that innocence. I remember the early Sixties for the hip action to the tune of Chubby Checker's "The Twist," and swoon-worthy Elvis "Pelvis" with his "Are you Lonesome Tonight?"

Some of my early letters to Otto aren't available, but my frustration is quite clear in his response to me. In one instance, I had been railing about sibling rivalry. My younger sister, Laura, was my nemesis. Popular, beautiful, straight A-super smart, she was everything I longed to be. I poured my heart to Otto, and he responded in turn:

Basel 6/19/59
Well, I just want to say, that it is quite normal, that sisters or brothers quarrel together at times, and so did Margot and Anne...The main thing is to know, that you intend the best, even if opinions differ. Your sister is still very young and so are you. Life is not always gay and I hope that later on, one will be a support for the other in every difficulty which may occur.

His words were true. Laura is a dear friend today. It was also during that time that I made Otto some cufflinks. I can't believe I had the gall to consider myself a jeweler, but Otto seemed genuinely pleased. He also talked about a passion of his. He would mention this throughout our correspondence:

June 7, 1960
...I am interested in youth all over the world and their problems. For this purpose I stimulated the establishment of the International Youth Center of the Anne Frank Foundation in Amsterdam with the aim to foster understanding between young people and to work with them in Anne's spirit against discrimination of all kinds.

Years later, I would discover how deeply committed Otto was to this cause. But now I was fifteen, and thoroughly involved with me and my active imagination. I wanted to be an actress and a dancer and asked Otto what I should do. His answer made a huge impact on my life:

7

Basel, 7/1960

As I see you are seriously thinking what to do later, I appreciate your confidence very much asking my opinion. I can understand your desire to become an actress and dance, but considering all you wrote me I think, that you should not make this the goal of your life. Continue to study dancing, continue to work on literature and drama, but let it be your private hobby.

There are many amateur groups, very good ones, too, so you always will be able to appear on the stage, if you continue to feel like. But to have acting and dancing as a job is very different. Even if you are talented, it affords continuous work from morning to night, you cannot have a real family life, you must give up privacy. A famous figure is in the light of the world (like Royalties), always considering: what will the public say or think of me. No, I would not wish this for you. I have a nephew, who is a star in "Holiday on Ice." He is traveling all over in the world, he has a good time—but must renounce his family life. He is more than happy, if he has a vacation and can stay with us "at home," he cannot marry and have a home for himself. Many of his colleagues did, but in most cases it is not a success. So I have to join those of your friends who are not in favor of your idea.

From what you wrote, I feel that you are a good hearted girl. You should not worry too much yet about your future. In growing up you certainly will be able to make the right choice.

You ask about my life. I am remarried and we are living her in the same house with my married sister and her family. We have a lot of correspondence and I am busy to organize in Amsterdam an Anne Frank International Youth Center. Therefore we are traveling a great deal.

I have to read a lot to be informed about Youth Movements and pedagogical questions and in our spare time we like to walk in the wonderful surroundings. We also study Italian.

This is all for today. I hope to have answered your questions and am wishing you and your family all the best.

Yours,

Otto Frank

This was the first time Otto mentioned his wife, though not by name. Otto had married Elfriede "Fritzi" Geiringer eight years after the war. He was introduced to her by Fritzi's daughter, Eva, as they were traveling by train from the concentration camps back to Amsterdam. Fritzi had lost her husband and son in the camps. The mother and daughter had survived against tremendous odds. And now, the young girl was excitedly pointing to the familiar man in the crowded train. "That's Mr. Frank! He's the father of my friend, Anne!" Eva and Anne had been playmates in the neighborhood, and Otto and Fritzi had never met until that point. Eva introduced the two, and after a long friendship and courtship, around seven years later, in November, 1953, Otto and Fritzi were married.

In careful, large script I answered "Mr. Frank"—I was calling him that, for we were rather formal in our respect for each other in those early years. Also, I seemed to write to him as in a foreign tongue—in very convoluted sentences, carefully screening out my young personality and presenting myself far more seriously than I really was.

A year later after a flurry of postcards to each other, I referred to his advice. I was still in high school.

My Dear Mr. Frank,

...In your last letter you might not recall this, but you answered my letter in which I asked your advice about my future as becoming an actress. Your opinion is one I shall remember and will greatly consider. You told me to join a drama group either in school or outside and not depend on becoming so much well famed as becoming a good person and raising a happy home.

Amen! Although my parents told me the same thing, somehow it's just that third someone to get the point across completely and cause me to seriously take heed to what has been explained to me. I'm obnoxious, I know! Seriously, your advice was more than I could ask for and I thank you for taking the time to consider my plea in the midst of your own worries. I've joined drama class at my school, dearly love every minute of it and you were absolutely right! I was in a Shakespeare Festival at the University of

California and the experience was one I shall never forget! I wish you and Mrs. Frank would have seen the excellent acting that the kids my age displayed—it was so exciting!

Before I end this letter I just wanted to ask how your work with the German youths has been coming along. Do you think that I could help by writing to them giving them some insight of the American Jewish teenager? Or in that matter do you think that the American teenagers could help in any way? If we could help you in some way lift the curtain of prejudice and ignorance than many of the German people have gained from lack of knowledge about the Jews or the Nazi Regime, would it be your opinion a great step in the sway of peace without prejudice? I would love to hear from you.

Always,
Cara Weiss

Mr. Frank answered this last part in a little note to me:

It will interest you to know that work at the Int. Youth Center is progressing and groups of young people from different countries are coming there to attend conferences and to have discussions.

With kindest regards—very sincerely Yours,
Otto Frank

It was during this time that I starred in my high school play, *Our Town*, as the character Emily—truly a high point in my life. I'd fallen in love with George, the male lead character, played by Tony LaRocco, a worldly and beautiful boy who I remember looking like George Chakiris in West Side Story. I also recall how he laughed at the fact that I didn't know how to kiss. He was right, but I don't think he knew how in love that Emily (a.k.a. Cara) was with George (Tony!) To this day, I have Emily's last speech in my office, and whenever I need a good cry I recite it out loud, convinced that I've just given an Oscar performance. It's a message embracing the simplicity of life—the beauty of those things we take for granted. It humbles me every time I read it:

"It goes so fast. We don't have time to look at one another. I didn't real-
ize. So all that was going on and we never noticed. Take me back—up the
hill—to my grave. But first: Wait! One more look. Good-by, good-by, world.
Good-by, Grover's Corners…Mama and Papa. Good-by to clocks ticking…
and Mama's sunflowers. And food and coffee. And new-ironed dresses and
hot baths…and sleeping and waking up. Oh earth, you're too wonderful for
anybody to realize you. Do any human beings ever realize life while they live
it?—every minute?"—Emily, from *Our Town,* by Thornton Wilder

Anyway, I was teetering on the brink of leaving the nest, and I
turned to Mr. Frank. He responded.

March 9, 1962
…I quite understand how you feel being seventeen years of age now. It
is natural that on one side you want to be independent and on the other
hand you are not yet enough sure of yourself so that you still need a certain
support. I only wish that you continue to appreciate the love and care you
found in your parents' home. It is one of the evils of American youth to try
to show an outside independence and to overlook the real values of life. It
seems to play a big role to have as many dates as possible and to be popular, neglecting a steady development of the character…How nice that you
enjoyed so much playing such an important role in Wilder's "Our Town."
We have seen the play some time ago and liked it immensely.

My letters continued as I babbled on about getting braces on my
bottom teeth as well as wondering about the futility of the world ar-
gued by some of my more scholarly pals who saw everything with such
a negative eye. I didn't want to focus on that and Otto agreed:

October, 1962
Dear Cara,
    …You are right not to take the bragging of the boys about nega-
tivism too serious. It is a fashion and the age, that makes them doubt

all values—but they will grow out! Follow your own conscience and conviction and have a positive standpoint in life. It will give you more satisfaction and firmness. Kindest regards, also from my wife, and love

Yours,

Otto Frank

In 1962-63 the political scene was a cauldron beginning to stew and boil over. Federal troops were sent to the University of Mississippi to force the school to enroll black James Meredith. Troops remained at the university until Meredith graduated in 1963. Here, one man had to fight for his dignity just to graduate—a black man in a white world. And I knew nothing of such pain or indignity facing my own graduation.

...I'm no longer "little!" I'm going to graduate high school this February and then I'll be a college girl! Can't believe it—just can't! I'm going to be eighteen soon and even that thought kind of shakes me up! So much for shocking realizations...

Jan. 21, 1963

Dear Cara,

...Just a few lines to thank you for your last letter and to wish you all the best for your exam...I am glad that you feel more grown-up now and am anxious to know how you will like College life. You'll make new friends and get interested in many items.

Good luck and kindest regards,

Yours,

Otto Frank

I was now attending Valley Junior College. My grades weren't good enough to go straight to a university, and frankly, the small size of Valley's campus was a perfect way to ease me into mainstream university life. I was very happy.

2-28-63

My Dear Mr. Frank—

I am now in college! I truly can't believe it—it has opened a whole new world to me. I've met the most fascinating, challenging people—and I suddenly am overwhelmed with a wonderful new sense of freedom! I love growing up—each new day offers such excitement. I often feel as if I'm on the brink of something terribly mysterious or unusual. If this feeling accomplishes anything at all—it simply keeps me in an optimistic frame of mind! In college I am taking Anthropology, Psychology, Spanish, Theatre Arts and Modern Dance. My favorite is Psychology. I still disagree with a certain Dr. Freud though! Personally I think the man was mentally warped and terribly frustrated! The nerve of him making a simple dream into a complex, symbolic monster! His theories I could do without!

…People who know that I am corresponding with you constantly ask so many questions about you. I take such pride in enlightening them with such a small bit of knowledge of the dear gentleman I've grown to love.

Last semester my high school put on the moving production of the story of your Anne. Mr. Frank, your whole family, as well as Anne will remain immortal in the hearts of peoples of the world. What a warm glow you must have within you to realize that.

I hope this letter finds both you and Mrs. Frank in high spirits and good health.

I am enclosing my graduation picture for you.

With warmest thoughts and wishes—

Cara

April 2ⁿᵈ 1963

Thank you for your enthusiastic letter and the photo. I compared the latter with snapshots you sent me in former years, you certainly changed. Growing up is exciting—if you are aware of it. Not all young people are though! They just live without thinking really about it. I am glad you are feeling fine and happy in your studies even if you do not like the Freud theory.

...I was glad to hear that your High School performed the Diary and I hope that they succeeded in conveying to the audience something of Anne's spirit. Sometimes I have the impression, that it is played, as any other play—and forgotten.

I am going to Amsterdam nearly every month, it is difficult to build an organization and I have a lot to do. At present we are preparing a pamphlet and as soon as it is ready I'll send it to you.

With all good wishes—as always yours

Otto Frank

It was 1963, the year of *To Kill a Mockingbird*, my most cherished movie of all—and the march for racial equality by two hundred thousand people in Detroit. The waves of protests in Birmingham, Alabama in April and May gained tremendous support for the civil rights movement. Police resorted to dogs and fire hoses to break up the demonstrations. It was horrifying to watch on television—I couldn't believe it was real. I'd never seen people treated like that in my life. What was happening to the world?

It was during this time that I remember talking for hours to my father and telling him I thought all religions just separated people; I was interested in causes, and I was ready to join Martin Luther King in Alabama and march with him and his people. I felt so helpless and lost. I just didn't understand how my temple and my people weren't more involved in integration, because it seemed that all the rabbi ever talked about was Israel. In truth, most of the leaders involved in integration on all levels were Jews and I slowly began to realize this. Then the horror began escalating until the impossible happened. Medgar Evers, the field secretary for the NAACP, was shot and killed in June.

And on November 22, the worst nightmare of all: President John F. Kennedy was killed by Lee Harvey Oswald in Dallas, Texas. Could this really be happening? I stood riveted under the campus loudspeaker as it announced the end of Camelot: President Kennedy has been shot in an assassination attempt..."

23.11.63

Dear Cara,

...We also were shocked deeply by the murder of Pres. Kennedy and we do feel his loss for the world. He was an extraordinary personality, whom we admired and loved...

Yours,

Otto Frank

I sent Otto an edition of *The Family of Man*—a photo essay on the human condition throughout the world. He was moved by the book and by my emotional dedication I wrote on the front of it.

February 19, 1965

Dear Cara,

...As each one of us has had hardships and sorrows, we feel grateful to have found each other and though we shall never forget the past and our dear ones, we achieved to have a positive outlook on life. In this attitude it is a great support to have still family, especially my wife's daughter, her husband and their 3 little girls (living in England) and devoted friends. Besides there are the daily reactions to the Diary of Anne which show me that she has not lived in vain and the work connected with the Anne Frank Foundation, Amsterdam.

...Thanks again and warmest regards to you and your dear ones in which my wife joins.

Yours,

Otto Frank

In those days, the Beatles were bigger than God, it seemed. They stormed the music scene, leaving Beatlemania in their wake. The world had never seen or heard anything like them. Everybody's hair got longer as soon as those mop tops hit the States. The "flower child" look started around this time—blue jeans with T-shirts and long hair. Wire-framed glasses were "in." So were miniskirts and body painting, knee designs of painted or pasted butterflies instead of stockings, along with beads, feathers, and sandals.

I took up the guitar and was singing at "hootenannies"—a real folkie like my heroes, Judy Collins; Joan Baez; Buffy Saint-Marie; Peter, Paul and Mary; Pete Seeger. The top radio hits then are still some of my favorites today: from those dazzling Brits, The Beatles "Yesterday,"; Petula Clark's "Downtown,"; "Mrs. Brown, You've got a Lovely Daughter", by Herman's Hermits; "Satisfaction" by the Rolling Stones; The Righteous Brothers' "You've Lost That Lovin' Feeling,"; and "I Got You, Babe," by Sonny and Cher.

I had graduated from Valley and was now attending UCLA. The following letter sounds deliriously happy. I don't remember it that way at all. Strange.

February 2, 1965

...I am now living at UCLA—it is a tremendous university with around 25,000 students—I'm so nothing here—and yet I'm so happy!

I'm 20 minutes from home—I talk to my family practically every day—we write—my parents try to come to the dormitory as often as possible—and still on my own! I entered this new world February, Mr. Frank. I have met, and am constantly meeting new, stimulating, intelligent people. I have decided I think that I would like to teach dramatics in high school. I'm majoring in Theatre Arts and minoring in English. My classes are like electricity, they are so thrilling! Our room is adorable—my roommate, Rita, is an English major and we share many hours with talk about authors, pets, and that wonderfully universal subject—boys!

Not to digress from this prevailing subject in my life---I wanted to tell you that I saw you on the television program "Twentieth Century" and was very moved by your words. I saw you and heard you for the first time and so wanted to really speak with you. I admired the strength and conviction in your whole presentation. The point that you brought up about Anne expressing the fact that although she said that she believed that there was good in all people, she was still young and full of youthful naivete about life and people. She certainly must have realized that there existed some persons without any true, deep goodness from within. It is only now, at the age of 20, do I now put people off their pedestals and accept the world without the rose colored glasses. I find that what I see now, is maybe not as beautiful, but it is human and real and Life—not fairyland.

I hope that your work and the ideals of Anne will indeed unite the curious, knowledge-seeking youth of today—and leaders of tomorrow...

July 28, 1965

Dear Cara,

I can imagine that your new life at the university changed your whole outlook and that your studies are most stimulating. You are very lucky that you have such a nice room-mate with who you can exchange your views and also that, though you are now on your own, you can keep close contact with your family.

...Please tell your cousin and his friends that we are still remembering their visit with pleasure and we could understand very well that during their European trip they like to look a little adventurous. We surely would not recognize them without beards.

As to my interview on TV I must tell you that I thought it was my duty to cooperate, though it was difficult for me to speak about the past. By the way, I have been asked to write an article for *Ladies' Home Journal* about Anne, which I did. It probably will be published in fall.

CHAPTER 3
Love and Marriage

Otto Frank was there for me when I changed college majors as fast as I changed socks. From dance to drama to English, my dear Basel "guidance counselor" was much more tolerant than my UCLA counselors. He listened and responded when I pondered the meaning of "greatness", wanting to be a playwright, and most of all falling in love with a Christian man I adored, Kent Wilson. I turned to Otto wondering about the possibility of a mixed marriage. That was when I turned twenty-one...

February 11, 1966

Dear Cara,

It is not easy to answer your last, long and detailed letter. I appreciate very much that you are writing to me in such an open-hearted and confidential way. You think that you have not become more mature though you are now twenty-one, but my impression is that you developed gradually anyhow. You cannot notice a change from one day to the other.

Whereas you had not made up your mind last year in which direction your study should lead you, you see how much clearer that your interest for everything connected with theater is a lasting one. If you feel that you can achieve something in writing plays, you certainly did the right thing in following courses on this subject. Perhaps psychology would be useful too. But in courses you only can learn the technical side. You will need a lot of experience in all sorts of human problems and relationships. So in leaving a job as secretary of a writer, or work in a publishing firm to become an editor or go into journalism, perhaps with the view to write play-critics.

If you really have the gift to become a good playwright, it will break through. Do not forget however that everyone with ambition is hoping for greatness—or at least success, which is not the same. Even if someone produces something great, it is frequently not recognized directly. But a real work of greatness survives generations.

Now to the great news that you are in love. I am so glad that you found a person with whom you have so much in common, whom you admire and who reciprocates your feelings. I am sure this love makes your life richer, but I fully understand your problem. My older brother married a non-Jewish girl. Both were not religious, but anyhow my sister-in-law offered to become Jewish, but my brother did not think it necessary, the more as they had no children. A year ago my nephew, who is an actor at the theater in Basel also married a gentile, a darling girl we all love very much. She had been an actress too, but gave up her career. They too are not religious and I am pretty sure that if they will get a child, it will not be baptized. In both cases the difference in religion and education did not influence in any way their life. To my idea there is one most important question. If your friend is deeply believing in Jesus as the son of GOD and the MESSIAH, I regard it as a great obstacle. This would always hurt your feelings and would create the greatest difficulties in the education of children. But if his belief is based more or less on the ethical principles of Christianism, then I do not see why you should not find a harmonious way of married life, as these principles are in fact based on the Jewish laws. Of course it needs much understanding from both sides anyhow. It surely would be good if you would get some books about progressive Judaism for your friend to read—from one of the may libraries of conservative or reform synagogues...

5/15/66

My Dear Mr. Frank—

Your letter in which you gave me such beautiful advice about mixed marriages and my career is a prize possession of mine. You gave me much deep thoughts to digest and dissect. It was certainly encouraging of you to relate the incidents of intermarriage in your own family. Marriage is still way up there on the pedestal. It is still intangible, unreal, and not foreseen in the near future. You have to know yourself and find security within your own self before you can ever hope to be a strength to a loved one. I haven't yet found that contentment.

I hope some day I can relax with myself, because when that day comes, I will be ready to accept the responsibility of marriage. Thank you so much, Mr. Frank, for your optimistic words on this topic. I don't know if I can yet accept such optimism.

I'm finding growing up, being a woman, beautiful and a little frightening. I'm not sophisticated where I can't still find a good cry or a strong, warm shoulder, or a call from home, a great source of pleasure and comfort.

How I would love to talk to you! To see you, to walk around the streets and sights that are yours. There is so much yet that I've to learn from you. How do you maintain a constant degree of objectivity when all the world is groveling in cruelty, hypocrisy, selfishness? Do I stand up on a soap box and Billy Graham them, or do I roll with the punch and hate myself the rest of my life for have a backbone made of jelly? Do I let my hair grow long, wear black tight boots and picket while all the little people turn their backs and complain how terrible the rest of the world is? I admit, I have a growing desire to vent my anger, my thoughts.

Yes, I still want to be a writer, but I've decided not to associate with the showbiz writers, the fast talkers, smooth movers, synthetic aesthetes. They are a discouraging dime a dozen, and I've discovered by some disenchanting experiences that I want no part of them. I've come to encounter many meaningful discoveries, ephiphanies as Joyce's Stephan Dedalus in Portrait of an Artist as a Young Man, had so called his daily realizations. And one of them is my love for you. I feel that you are so a part of my life. I don't like to undress my thought waves to many people, so I have garbed them in letter form to you. And through the years you have closted them and made me feel that you've believed in me. I can't thank you enough for sharing your thoughts, your philosophy with me. Anne knew in an annex what has taken me six rs to grow to know about you. I feel very fortunate.

To just fill you in on newsy news I'll tell you the latest in these here parts. My roommate, Rita, graduated from college last week! It was a beautiful ceremony, and it gave me inspiration that should last me for at least another year when, glory of glories, I'll be set free! My sister, Laura, graduates tomorrow night! She is speaking at her graduation and practically is walking off with every honor conceivable! (It's times like this that I wonder if I was adopted...)

My parents, God bless them, are well and wonderful. They have kept us starving students fed with their surprise overabundance of groceries every time they come to visit us! Rita and I are working at Bank of America and truly love it! The people are from all walks of life, from every status group and practically every nation and creed. It's actually just a miniature U.N.!

Our apartment is adorable: tiny, glowing, orange and turquoisy, filled with odd shaped bottles (I collect them), guitars, (we both play), albums (folk, classical, musicals, movie themes), here a collage with bright colored clippings and paraphernalia with a progressive, fringing on hostile poem (written by guess who), books and magazines, more bottles (I said I loved them), some artistic photographs of children (taken by an artist friend of Rita's), a cupboard without a door, (the manager said that the cabinet-maker said that there would be a detainment of his services because of the war in Viet Nam—now really, that gullible we are not!), also a leaky faucet, a telephone that dials itself, (really, I was alone when it started to dial from the inside, and when it finished I was already begging forgiveness for being the devil's advocate—I thought sure the gods were going to get me this time! And letters, cards and pictures. I wish you could see it. I wish I could see you!

8/19/66

Mr. Frank!

I missed you so!! I hope that you and Mrs. Frank are well—please if you have a moment, scribble out a bit of note to me. I must talk to you soon! Mr. Frank, you don't know how much I think of you and value our brief, newsy written thoughts across the miles. I've always cherished a constant dream of some day meeting you, but too much school and not enough money have kind of burst that bubble. Our letters have made the broken daydream of a lovely alternative though so please don't stop talking to me!!!

...I'm feeling much more optimistic since our last talk, but then this is still today, and tomorrow is yet to come...Knock on wood, spit three times and hold your breath—with God's help—I'll be graduating either in March or June of '67 and I can't wait! I aspire to go into advertising—it's a very hard, competitive field, but I'm keeping my fingers crossed that I can be hard and competitive right back! I'm still in love with Kent and hope with all my heart that that dream of eternal life with him will some day come true. We have a lot against us—but even more for us...

26th August 1966

Dear Cara,

Before we went to England we spent a week in Amsterdam where we attended the International Youth Conference at the Anne Frank House. It was most interesting and stimulating and young people from 9 different countries took part. I suppose you received the programme and I am sure you would have been very much interested in the theme, "Is there a place for religion in the modern world." Most of the young people of different creeds were longing for something to believe in, but did in general not like the existing forms. But for me not only the lectures and discusses were important, but especially the personal contact. After the conference I received...a letter from a Jewish girl from England who met at the conference a young German boy. In getting to know him better she completely lost her prejudice against the Germans.

You wrote that you lost much of your idealism and that you are so sorry that the world is in such a mess and you ask me what my standpoint is in this respect. I know that a single person all by himself cannot bring about important changes, but nevertheless one should not be indifferent and everyone of us has the duty to do all his power to help join the forces of peace and understanding. That is why I believe in the Anne Frank Foundation and work for it.

I was glad to hear that your friendship with Ken gives you happiness though it involves many problems. Nevertheless it is surely right not to hasten developments and to have a long time of probation…

11-5-66

Dear Mr. Frank—

Your thoughts have a very soothing effect on me. My gentle German philosophic friend of seven years! Thank you for the strengthening effect you have on me as well. I am now supposed to be studying for an exam, but with the beautiful music that is playing, and the restlessness of my mind, my thoughts strayed to you.

I hope to graduate from the university in June—I'm truly looking forward to that eventful day…I'm in love—and I am loved—so what else is there to feel?! The world still troubles me—but I've realized that I guess I kind of trouble the world, too! After all, to my chagrin, I've discovered that I'm a people, too!

Kent and I are taking classes in Judaism every Tuesday evening and both love it! Thank you for your very valid advice in this matter. He doesn't realize that I've planned his reading material—(He'll be saying `Shalom' in his sleep!)…

The background of these benign meanderings was a gathering storm of fury. Vietnam was in full bloom. U.S. Troops numbered 389,000 by the end of 1966. Huey Newton and Bobby Sale formed the revolutionary Black Panther party in Oakland, California. The Chicago race riots hit big—it took 4,200 National Guardsmen and 533 arrests to stop the madness. And for the first nine months of `67, a total of 164 riots broke out in major cities causing one hundred deaths and over two thousand injuries. "The Ballad of the Green Berets," by Sgt. Barry Sadler, was played over and over again. Blacks were already wearing their hair Afro-style. Whites were wearing the long, straight dos. As I counted the months to graduation, I hummed along to Simon and Garfunkel's "Sounds of Silence," the Beatles' "Paperback Writer,", "Penny Lane," "All You Need is Love," the Doors' "Light My Fire," and the Rolling Stones' "Ruby Tuesday." During that time, there was a write-up saying that Otto Frank would be going to Munich to a trial against war criminals.

I sent my friend a telegram:

2-4-67
Some times are harder than others to believe that people are really good at heart. My love to you in a very hard time.

February 6, 1967
Dear Cara,

I was very much surprised when I received your cable this morning and thoroughly moved by your thoughtfulness. It was so sweet of you to show me in this way how strongly you are feeling with me.

I am writing you immediately because I want to tell you that the papers were wrong writing that I would go to Munich personally. I never thought of doing so and was only represented by my lawyer. Of course I am following everything up in the papers which is rather exciting and besides I have to answer many questions of journalists who want to know my opinion. Some are ringing up from abroad even from Moscow. You surely are right that those accused cannot be regarded as normal human beings, they worked like computers without heart or feelings. But now at least two of them show signs of repenting.

In all this lawsuit Anne is regarded as a symbol for all the unknown victims.

I hope you are well and happy and I suppose that you are very busy…

During the following time I did indeed graduate from UCLA in March, Kent and I were engaged and then married in July. My letter to my dearest mentor was filled with excitement as well as the challenge of Judaism vs Christianity and the support and non-support of others who just didn't think it would all work out. But we found a patient Rabbi who encouraged Kent to first study Judaism, while we both avidly researched the pros and cons of intermarriage. Plus I began working at Young & Rubicam, Inc. as a copy secretary for the copywriters. It was a busy time to say the least.

May 27, 1967
Dear Cara,

...Now first of all I want to thank you for the two lovely photos marking two important events of your life. Though your graduation is the high-point of your studies and certainly a great achievement, your engagement means a lot more for your future life.

Looking at the photo of you and Kent, your radiant happiness reflects upon us and we are sending to both of you our hearties congratulations.

I can imagine the big problems confronting you, but I know from all you have written how seriously both of you have thought about the question of the difference in religion. As you know I am very broad-minded and I understand that none of you wants to convert. It is a great blessing that both parents agree to your marriage and are a support for you. Do not mind the disapproval of others. The main thing is that your personalities are well matched and you have respect for each other's conviction. I am very glad that you are in agreement about the very important point of the religious education of your children, as this is in many cases the bases of difficulties.

I would be very interested to know the name of the Rabbi who showed so much understanding for your case. Of course we too would love to be present at your wedding, but you are right that this will not be possible. We wonder where you will settle down and we understand that this will depend on Kent's decision if he will continue his studies or accept a job.

You can imagine how excited we are about the situation in the Middle East. I am deeply worried and depressed to the aggression of the Arab States behavior of its so-called friends who do not take any action. For me Nasser is following the example of Hitler, both have openly propagated their plans and the world has not reacted until it was too late.

If Israel is not helped very soon and the solemn promise of the Allies that the gulf of Akaba will remain a free international water-way is not kept, then Nasser will go on with his intention to destroy Israel.

I am sorry that my letter is ending in such a gloomy way, but I know that you will understand my feelings…

3-68

Dear Cara and Kent,

At the occasion of your first wedding anniversary, my wife and I are sending you best wishes. We are happy that you are happy.

Warmest regards and love,

Yours,

Otto Frank

March 26, 1968

Dear Cara and Kent,

Time flies and though I wanted to answer your dear letter sooner, I just did not find the leisure. When I read your heartwarming reminiscences about our relationship since so many years and how you are valuing it, I was really moved. Now I want to tell you that the confidence you always had in me was a precious gift from your side. Having contributed a little to your development, gives me satisfaction…I was extremely glad to hear that you and Kent are so happy together…

…I have great respect for your Rabbi who was so broad-minded to respect Ken's religious feelings not insisting on his conversion. Though you both adhere to your own religions, you manage to celebrate holidays meanfully.

Now about us. We had a wonderful winter-vacation in the mountains together with the children and grandchildren from England, who are always a great joy for us. This did us a lot of good and we stayed in good shape during the winter. I am still very active, going to Amsterdam nearly every month and working regularly daily on my correspondence together with my wife. In spring and summer we are expecting a lot of visitors from abroad.

In May however we shall be in London for some time and in July we are going to attend the Int. Youth Conference in Amsterdam as every year. The theme this time will be "Youth and Human Rights." In case you know some students or other young people who are going to Europe and may be interested to attend, it would be nice to draw their attention to it.

You know that the aim of the Foundation is to further understanding and to work for peace; though the state of world affairs is very discouraging, we must not give up. Anyhow we are very worried about the situation in Vietnam, for which we do not see any solution and about the tension between black and white in your country. We are following everything very closely and we are very sad about the decrease of prestige and economical power of the United States. This influences also, we are sorry to say, the position of Israel, as America is not able to back it sufficiently.

We only hope that another president will be elected who will be able to run things to the better…

CHAPTER 4

Political and Social Awakening

The year 1968 was etched in my mind. I can't ever forget it. Otis Redding was "Sittin' on the Dock of the Bay"…while we hummed along to "Hey Jude" by the Beatles…and "I Heard it Through the Grapevine" by Marvin Gaye…and then the world stopped. On April 4th in Memphis, Martin Luther King was killed by James Earl Ray. And on June 5th in the Ambassador Hotel in Los Angeles, Bobby Kennedy was killed in front of the world by Sirhan Sirhan. The young senator had just won the California Democratic presidential primary.

June 6, 1968

Dear Mr. Frank—

"America! America! God Shed His Light on Thee!" Today, Mr. Frank, I don't know whether I can ever sing that song and still believe in those words. I don't want to turn my back on the land I've loved so fiercely, but the foundation, the "free"soil beneath my feet is shaken. I'm frightened. And angry. And ashamed. And terribly lost in the poisonous atmosphere of fear…and hate. Bobby Kennedy is dead. Martin Luther King is dead. John F. Kennedy is dead. Medgar Evers is dead. All shot by the bullets of madmen. Madmen who at some time in their sad lives cried out to their neighbors for help…and no one heard…or cared. Lonely men with scapegoats to vent their sick self-hate upon.

Bobby Kenned. A saint? No. A Christ? No. No. No. A Man. A man with youth and anger. A quick-silver mind and a body. A man not afraid of the mud or the darkness or the complexity of the ghetto or the slick city. A man that Charles Evers, the brother of the slain Medgar Evers, believed in. The only white man he really trusted. And his feelings were echoed by the majority of the black people. Bobby Kennedy. A father and a husband and a brother and a son and the only hope for peace in the minds of millions all over the world.

Yes, the gentle, wise Senator Eugene McCarthy is a man I can believe in as well. Robert Kennedy wanted to unite with this man. He believed that together, their philosophies and their followers would bring peace to our broken nation, to our broken world.

Where do I go now, Mr. Frank? Must I love and believe in my world with the paranoid distrust and defense mechanism that involves no real commitment? To play it safe and not love…because then I'll not be crushed? But then I won't have lived totally…wholly…will I? When your world was destroyed…how did you go about repairing it? How can I help strengthen the world that is falling around me? I can't cradle my crying nation to my breast andnurse it back to health. But I want to. I can't storm the U.N. and shake each man by his shoulders and beg him to tear down the walls. But I want to. I can't stand in the middle of our land and scream for everyone to run and touch his neighbor's face…white hands on black cheek bones and vice-versa…see the loneliness in each other's eyes…hear the whisper before the scream…and the gunshot. But I want to. Will we ever see into each other's eyes? The beautiful American Indians…stony-faced and quiet in the silence of their neglected, unjust worlds. And the Mexican-Americans… their vibrancy stifled by crowded quarters…away from the big cities.

How can I bring a child into this world? What can I promise him? Freedom? Peace? Love? Tolerance? Tomorrow? I don't mean to be embittered. Or reject the substance, the core of living that these great men died for in their fight for peace.

Bobby Kennedy is gone. And he was so briefly here. Just beginning to convince us of a peaceful tomorrow.

And I was just beginning to break down my defenses. To extend my hand to him. To be vulnerable in my love and respect for him. Tuesday I voted for him. As did the majority of people here, because he won the primary race in California. And then a madman decided he was too great to contain any longer. And he killed RFK.

Thank God Kent and I have each other during this mentally and emotionally trying ordeal. We want to be strong. We don't want to give up and forget what Bobby awakened within us. Kent has helped me. When I start to strike out and hate the hate, he reminds me of the power of love.

You are a forgiving man. A man of strength and inner battle scars. I could us some of your moral plasma right now. I would like to help you, Mr. Frank, in the way you've helped me. I would like to write a pamphlet or essay extending the philosophy and love of Anne Frank. Your found is a beginning. A great attempt to reach the youth of the world and give them hope. Today's youth needs hope. They need to believe in tomorrow. Not enough people know about your foundation. Let me help you awaken their knowledge of you and your work. Do you want this of me?

I feel a little better now, as I always do once I've "talked" to you. And as you also know, I love you. Please tell me what is the date of your birth. I know it was sometime in May, but you never let me know. I promise I won't embarrass you with a huge Cecil B. DeMille production. I just want to know. Since I'm already late, I wish you much health and happiness and a happy, happy birthday and many, many more!!!!

Please, Mr. Frank, don't think I'm rejecting my America. I love my country. My people. I just feel so helpless now. At this moment, I can't see any shedding light. I feel so empty. Along with your prayers, Mr. Frank, please include America. Thank you for listening, dear friend. God Bless You.

Much love, Cara

June 16, 1968
Dear Cara,

Your last letter written under the impression of the shock you felt after the assassination of Robert Kennedy moved me very much. It was not a letter—it was an outcry. I understood you so well as I share in many respects your feelings. I too, as well as millions in the whole world are mourning over the death of R. Kennedy and those before him who became victims of fanatics. They all were excellent men on whom the hope of many good-willing people was set upon. If the murderers acted out of personal grievances, one could not blame "America" for these crimes, but one cannot help to be suspicious that powerful, evil groups are working behind the screens. If this is really the case and they can extend their power and succeed in eliminating the progressive forces, I see the future of America very gloomily.

If nothing will be done to end the Vietnam war and to help the poor and neglected masses, there really is the danger of an uprising, a civil war. The pathetic words of Rev. Abernathy addressing the crowds at the march of the poor, that this is the last chance of a peaceful solution, makes one shudder. But there is still an alternative. There are millions who are feeling their responsibilities just as you do.

In your democratic system there is the possibility of influencing affairs by election. Much will depend on the next President and his advisers. As far as we can judge from here however, not one of the candidates can replace Kennedy. Though McCarthy has about the same aims, he seems not to have the brilliant, energetic personality, but one must hope that he will grow with his duties, should he be elected. Or should the republican party be given a chance with Rockefeller? Though the situation is far from satisfactory, you must not be desperate. Never give up!

I remember to have once read a sentence, "If the end of the world would be imminent, I still would plant a tree today." When we lived in the secret annexe we had the advice "Fac et spera" which means: "Work and hope." I do not know if I ever wrote this to you.

So you should not ask if you should bring a child into this world. Life goes on and perhaps your child will bring the world one step further. Anne who died as a victim of injustice and hatred, achieved something for mankind in her short life. Perhaps the new generation will live under quite different circumstances than we can imagine now and will have a quite different feeling of happiness.

You are right that at certain periods of my existence the world around me collapsed. When most of the people of my country, Germany, turned into hordes of nationalistic, cruel anti-Semitic criminals, I had to face the consequences and through this did hurt me deeply I realized that Germany was not the world and I left forever.

When I returned from the concentration camp alone, I saw that a tragedy of unexpressible extent had hit the Jews, my people, and I was spared as one of them to testify, one of those who had lost his dear ones.

It was not in my nature to sit down and mourn. I had good people around me and Anne's Diary helped me a great deal to gain again a positive outlook on life. I hoped by publishing it to help many people in the same way and this turned out to be true.

When later the Anne Frank Foundation was established I wanted it to work in the spirit of Anne's ideals for peace and understanding among peoples.

But as you can imagine we are working on a rather small scale as we only can reach and try to influence people who are coming to the Anne Frank House. It was always my wish to make it to the center of an international organization with branches in many countries, which would have to deal with their specific problems. Up to now this was not possible.

You are asking me what you could do to spread the hope which is contained in Anne's Diary to the benefit of the youth of your country. Maybe that through a pamphlet, as you propose it, an action could be started and an Anne Frank group formed. This group should issue a paper in which young people could express themselves freely, trying to find positive answers to the many-fold problems which divide America.

U.S.A. has the sad reputation to have the highest rate of crime and dope in the world. Why not fight against the horror and crime films and literature? I know that big business wold oppose the oppression of such films. Ammunition and war material industries are against the limiting of the sale of weapons. Only youth with ideals could take a stand against these evils. This is just one idea.

But how could such a paper be financed and distributed? I am thinking of subscription and many voluntary helpers.

I am so glad that you have Kent at your side in these difficult times. He gives you strength and comfort. The harmony between you should enable you to cope with every situation. I hope that the opportunities he got by winning a scholarship will prove to be fruitful for him.

Please excuse my English. Of course I could express my thoughts better in my own language.

Let me thank you for your good wishes for my birthday. It was on May 12th.

Write again if you feel like it. My wife and I are sending our love to you and Kent,

Yours,

Otto Frank

8/27/68

Dear Mr. Frank:

Without sounding too gushy, I have to say that you're wonderful. Your letter in answer to mine after Robert Kennedy's death meant more than I can begin to express. You gave me encouragement. A little of your philosophy. You gave me inspiration to plant that tree today...even when my strongest intuition tells me there will be no tomorrow.

What would I do without you, dear friend? My Kent found strength from your letter, too. He thinks so much of you. And what a wonderful surprise to have you remember our anniversary! You and Mrs. Frank are beautiful people! We couldn't believe a whole year had passed already. And we still like each other. Amazing! As anniversary gifts to each other, we exchanged albums we made for one another. I made an album of all the little mementoes and pictures collected from our courtship days, and Kent made one of our whole first year. Kent's really great. He's so artistic and such a perfectionist! I wish you could see the albums. The house reeked of glues for days after our massive projects, but the end result paid off. Two sentimental nuts.

The world situation is still as miserable as it was yesterday and the day before. The situation in Czechoslovakia is very depressing. I pray that those strong people won't give up their fight for freedom…no matter what. I had such hope for their success. And our up-and-coming elections are a farce. I've never seen or heard or felt such confusion in my life. Can you imagine people actually taking Nixon and Maddox and Wallace seriously? It's frightening. People (and I don't mean to deny my claim to peopleness) never cease to amaze me. They hear and see only what they want to. Fear blinds and deafens them. They all want to do "the right thing" and they think that by closing their doors and windows to the world they're doing just that.

Kent and I are going to join the American Civil Liberties Union dedicated to aiding minorities or impoverished peoples. It's very powerful out here and from what we've heard from talking to some very fine people, very successful as well. Our white America also has to be elevated. There have been a series of documentaries each week on Black America. They have been brilliant and very moving as well as shocking. I'm ashamed of my ignorance after being enlightened of the extensive subtle cruelty and degradation done to the black man in America. I'm tired of shaking my head in disbelief. I've got to do something. Now.

I wonder, and this is what I've been meaning to ask you: do the majority of temples in America know about the foundation? When I asked a woman who is in charge of the Jewish organization at U.C.L.A. called Hillel if she knew about the foundation, she didn't know about it and wondered if you have any kind of plan to awaken these youth organizations as well as temples and churches about the foundation and the summer conferences. She was very enthusiastic about it and said she would help in any way she could. Do you want me to compile some sort of general list of these organizations, write a standard letter of introduction and then you could include all the information you wanted to about the foundation? Please let me know. I want to help you.

What I would love more than anything in the world, is to meet you. Just the other day I told Kent that I would love to write a book—a biography about you. Kent said that the only way I could really do that would be if I met you. And I said I know. I think that people should know you. You owe society the secret of your wondrous philosophy of life. I'm sure you have been asked this before. But this is just one of my Number One dreams. If we could work some way out of interviewing via tapes…but then I wouldn't see your expression…the way you held your hands…turned your head…

Well, from the state that this letter is in, you'd never know I'm an executive secretary. (Not for long I hope. Last week I started going on interviews at different advertising agencies. I'm looking for a writing position.)…

I didn't mention this in my letters to Otto, but during this time I journeyed to San Francisco with my friend Nancy Gerston, carrying tons of deli goods, blankets, and high hopes of joining forces with the Native Americans on Alcatraz Island. What I'd hoped to accomplish I'm not quite sure—and neither were they. Always a "Walter Mitty" dreamer, I think I saw myself as some kind of super-writer who would tell the world of the Native American's plight and save them all and then they would embrace me as their honorary Indian-in-residence. In truth, I met up with a ragtag group of tribal parties—having a party. They were not overjoyed with my presence and didn't think I looked one iota like a Native American (my blue eyes didn't help.) Buffy Sainte-Marie was nowhere to be seen. And not even one painted pony. My life has followed a pattern of disappointing scenarios like this. If I would just "Let It Be," as the Beatles sang…

September 27, 1968

Dear Cara,

In your last letter you mentioned that you are looking for a new, more creative job and I hope that you will find one which will give you more satisfaction and in which you can use your wonderful gift of expressing yourself in writing. It is always a pleasure for me to read your letters which show your whole lovable personality. Just as you would like to meet me, my wife and I would love to meet both of you. From our long correspondence you could perhaps make out that I do not like to be in the public eye and therefore it would be embarrassing for me if a book about me would be written. So please do not follow up this idea.

As to your suggestions about the Anne Frank Foundation, there are two aspects: one is to make it more widely known so that young people would visit the house when travelling in Europe to meet young people from other countries there and attend our International Summer Conference. It is not possible to propagate the Foundation and its aims from Amsterdam, so we should have a center in U.S.A. helping us in this respect. Our survey of activities for 1967 has just been published in Holland and is now being translated into English. As soon as it will be ready, I shall send you one and perhaps you think it worthwhile to send extracts of it to Temples and Church groups.

Then the Foundation badly needs financial help, as I have written you before. We are trying to make the Foundation tax exempt for U.S.A. knowing that substantial amounts will only be given if people can deduct them from their taxes. In principle I never wanted to ask Jewish organizations for financial help as I think their actions should be concentrated on Israel. As soon as we get a decision about our application I shall let you know.

Just as you we are deeply worried about the world situation. By the invasion of C.S.S.R. Russia has shown its true face and making use of the weakness of U.S.A. and the disagreement of Europe, is trying to extend its power. So the elections in your country affect all of us here in Europe and are of great importance in view of the situation in the Middle East. Whereas the Russians are backing the Arab States openly all the time America does not dare to do the same for Israel. So we only can hope that a new war can be prevented. One feels so powerless in the game of supernations...

As to us we had a pleasant holiday at the Belgian coast with two of the grandchildren from England. Later we went to London and I attended a conference of the World Congress of Faith where representatives of many religions took part. It will interest you to hear that there was also an all faith service…

In honor of my birthday that year, Otto Frank did the most incredible thing. He sent me a note that said this on it: "2 Trees in Israel in the name of Mrs. Cara Wilson for her birthday. Planted by Mr. O. Frank, Birsfelden."

In 1970, I was eating yogurt—the latest health craze—and buying only "organic" or "natural" foods, free of chemical fertilizers and pesticides. Funny, I never liked yogurt. Still, it was high on the "should" list. (Do we ever really like those "should" in our life?) The look was unisex and "hot pants"—those sexy, short shorts that we wore with platform shoes and a cute little cloche hat. I did all that. False eyelashes, too. I was also playing the guitar all the time. I considered being a singer/songwriter for about a blink. One song during those days has since become my own personal mantra—one that even talked to me in a prophetic dream: The Beatles' "Let It Be."

1970 was also the year when the Beatles disbanded, and the Chicago Seven caused such havoc. Jerry Rubin, Abbie Hoffman, Rennie Davis—the whole bunch of them were in the news for their rowdy, anti-establishment, ant-war antics during the 1968 Democratic National Convention. David Dellinger tired to hold a courtroom reading of the names of the Vietnam War dead. Once Rubin and Hoffman wore judicial robes during their trial and they passed out jellybeans. They screamed furious epithets at Judge Julius Hoffman. It was wild. Meanwhile, Vietnam was raging. Even though President Nixon announced his intention to withdraw additional 150,000 troops by the year's end, heavy U.S. bombing continued targeting North Vietnam in retaliation for their attacks on our reconnaissance flights.

By now Americans were made aware of a gruesome event—the My Lai massacre in March of '68. Over two hundred Vietnamese villagers were brutally killed by U.S. troops. Students and "peaceniks" all over the country were holding rallies to stop the war in Vietnam. I joined in and sang along as we held candles and cried, "All we are saying, is give peace a chance." And then on our own soil, we had our own massacre. Kent State...

5/5/70

Dear Mr. Frank:

...I don't have to reiterate what these sad, sick, violent events are—you know about them. The most recent tragedy is the death of four students killed on a campus in Ohio—shot in peaceful action. They were protesting an immoral war. The troops that were called in to stop the rally were young men, scared by flying rocks and scared by a situation they had no right stirring up. They shouldn't have had guns in their hands. Guns at an anti-war demonstration. Doesn't make sense, does it? There's so much sickness going on here, Mr. Frank. It's very hard to believe in planting trees today—who knows if there will be air for them to live in tomorrow? It's not the kind of world I would choose to raise a child in. But, I'm also selfish. If my life isn't going to be long, I don't want to die without experiencing the birth and raising of a child. Please forgive my pessimism, Mr. Frank, I don't mean to bombard you with these angry thoughts. I'm not giving up. I plan to use my writing as a weapon. There are organizations blooming around town that believe in pure air and peace and they need help selling these "products," both Kent and I plan to assist them. At least we'd feel we were doing something.

I wrote the following flyer for the Anne Frank Foundation in May 1970:

"What can we, young people, do to prevent such horrors and to create a livable world?" These words were repeated over and over again in the diary of a now very famous young woman, Anne Frank. Today, the words

*are echoed by the young in loud and impassioned voices. In a day of hostile
gaps separating generations and races and religions, there is a place were
everybody can get together. The Anne Frank Foundation.*

*Established May 3, 1957, in Amsterdam, the Foundation is a meeting
place for young minds to mix and grow. It has welcomed visiting individuals and groups from all over the world. It is not just for Jews. It is for peoples
of all religions. And political views. And the come in all colors. Visiting
professors, doctors, scientists, politicians and artists direct classes throughout
the year. The classes center around current topics. They are fresh and challenging and many times painful. They are beautiful.*

*The Anne Frank Foundation has survived because of a father's belief in
a daughter's belief. Mr. Otto Frank lives in Basel, Switzerland and spends
all his time furthering the growth of the Foundation. He believes that the
future of the world stands in the faith of the young: "Even if you feel there
is no tomorrow—you must plant a tree today."*

*The Anne Frank Foundation is a beautiful tree. And it is there for
young people to climb. No matter how old they are. For more information
on how you can attend or contribute to the Foundation, please write to:
The Anne Frank Foundation, Prinsengracht 263, Amsterdam."*

June 29, 1970
Dear Cara,

...We were glad to hear that you and Kent are satisfied with your
work and that you are happy together.

It would be wonderful if you could carry out your plan to come
to Europe next summer and that we could meet after having been in
contact with you for so many years.

Recently we had the visit of several young American friends and
they all were very unhappy about the situation in U.S.A. not only
about the war in Indochina, but also about the tendency to fascism
not only in the administration but also in a great part of the population. This really is frightening and a growing recession may stimulate
this movement. We have been told that everyone opposing this trend

is regarded as a communist. It is difficult to think of America as a free country any longer. Anyhow I just cannot imagine that there are not enough people who are realizing the danger and it is more important than ever that the positive forces join so that perhaps in the next election a change to the better can be brought about. Let us hope that in the meantime Israel will not become the victim of the bad and short-sighted American politics...

August 6, 1970
Dear Cara,
     ...We are longing for peace and justice and now there is a little spark of hope that settlement may be reached in the Middle East.

My tree of hope began to blossom. But not everyone's world was as beautiful as mine during that time. The Black Panthers—whom I had supported so passionately—were now becoming increasingly more violent. Their furious confrontations with the police were becoming widespread, and Panther leaders Fred Hampton and Mark Clark were killed in a dramatic Chicago police raid. And while I was shaking my fist in outrage, I was also patting my tummy...

CHAPTER 5

A New Life

September 16, 1970

Dear Mr. Frank:

Fantastic news! We're going to be parents! Kent and I are really excited by it all. I found out officially last week. The doctor confirmed my queasy stomach and said that there was a reason for it: I was around two months pregnant. I wish I could say that you and Mrs. Frank are the first to know, but I've been so thrilled about the news that I tell anybody and everybody I know and don't know. Everybody, that is, except where I work. We really can't afford my quitting at this stage, and I just hope I can hold off from saying anything for awhile. At least until nature starts showing off.

Meanwhile, on top of everything, we just bought a beautiful old house in the hills. It's got a world of trees and plants in abundance around it, lots of wood and stairs and something I've always wanted: an attic. There's quite enough room for you and Mrs. Frank when you come to visit us. So, we refuse to allow you to say no. We're planning on that day. And we're stubborn, you can't convince us otherwise. You've got to come and stay with us! It's the kind of house I know you'd love. We're painting it now. Tearing down things and building more. Kent's been working very hard. This is our first house. Our first baby. We're very lucky and very happy. When I think of all the traumas I've gone through growing up. I've written each stage, each peak of emotion, each aching age of recognition—maturity to you, dear friend.

I've never felt so good about people as I do now. My anger with them still sharpens my focus, but I find that I have more room for love than I ever did. Yes, the news does seem to get worse, but in subtle, gentler ways the people seem to get better. I am contradicting myself. I defended the Black Panthers. I stood behind Angela Davis. I believe in the rightful anger of the militant. And then they showed up backing the Arabs. I felt like shaking them. Screaming at them. They have judged the small, selfish ghetto Jew, the liquor store owner in Harlem, the grocery store merchant in Watts, the little man who has conned them and thrown them aside—they have judged this sad representation of a people and put all Jews in his category. They have overlooked all the hippie and yippie leaders—mostly Jews—who have fought alongside them. Who have raised their fists—their white, Jewish fists—high in the air next to the black fists. I think that the Black Panthers could do so much for their people and consequently for our country. Their anger could be used so beautifully. It could raise black egos out of their graves—out of their ghettos—into leadership. The blacks could lead white, silent majority, chalky, frightened America into greatness. They could kill ignorance with the first of their beautiful souls. But the Panthers make it very hard. They prefer personal power. I shake inside with anger and disappointment for them. And yet I love them still. Maybe my love will get to them some way or another. I'm not giving up.

Little Israel never will. American people are slowly realizing that the courage of that tiny country is giving us courage. I've got a lot to overcome. And we shall overcome. By God, we shall. I'm finding that in the pain of our existence, people are becoming closer together. Sensitivity groups are popping up everywhere. People want to touch each other and see the primitive, animal, purity in each other. They reach out.

Organized religions aren't filling this aching gap. They are too removed, too obscure, too alienated from the world, from the next handclasp. Pure spiritual religions, the original religions of the rebellious Moses, the forgiving Christ, the questioning Confucius, are emerging. This is what excites and challenges me and gives me some hope for my future child. This is the tree I know will be growing tomorrow. The tree of love. It was conceived with it. I pray it will grow tall with it—even after I'm gone.

October 15, 1970

Dear Cara,

What wonderful news your last letter brought us! From every line of it we can see how happy you are that you and Ken will have a baby.

Without having known that you are pregnant you bought the beautiful house in the hills in which your child will grow up. This must be more than sheer coincidence. We are wishing from the bottom of our heart that the future life of the Wilson family in their new home will be a happy one and though there will be ups and downs, we are sure that your mutual love will overcome everything.

There is only one thing we regret—that we shall not be able to have you with us here next summer, because you will not come to Europe as you had intended. Though you invited us so cordially there is no chance that we shall come to the States. Believe me I would love to be with you and Ken after we have been in correspondence for more than 11 years, following every phase of your development, but you forget that I have grown older too and am now 81. Though I am in good condition, I need a lot of rest and a visit to America where I have a great number of good friends would be too great a strain for me.

So I am afraid we shall have to wait until the three of you can come over. There are many young American couples who visit Europe with small children.

We can imagine that you and Ken have a lot of work repairing and painting the old house and shaping it according to your taste. But you surely love to do as much as possible yourselves as then it becomes more a part of you.

You are writing that your whole outlook on life has changed some-what since you know that you will be a mother. You see hopeful signs in developments and we agree that it is good if young people are taking an active part in trying to abolish injustices and all sorts of grievances. But we cannot follow your views regarding Black Panthers. Not only because they are backing the Arabs, disregarding true facts, but also because the leaders incite the whole movement to violence not for the good cause, but to get power. If they really would get it, they would misuse it and discriminate others. To my opinion problems cannot be solved by terrorism and violence...

November 17, 1970

Dear Mr. Frank:

Thank you for the lovely letter. It was so good hearing from you and Mrs. Frank. But don't write us off completely! We still plan on seeing you both as soon as possible. As soon as the baby appears and our first year house worries disappear, we'll know where we stand financially. And I hope it's close to you two. We're counting on it.

I am enclosing a confirmation service that will take place at my parents' temple. My father wanted to make sure you saw it, he thought you'd be pleased. The graduating youth from the temple will read the words of your Anne. It's a beautiful tribute to her and to their futures. If you feel like it—if you have time, you might want to either tape some sort of introduction to be heard at the evening, or a letter from you would be read at the congregation. If you don't want to, that's fine. Dad just wanted you to know about this evening. He's putting it together and is very excited about it...

November 28, 1970

Dear Cara,

Thank you very much for your kind letter and the text for a confirmation service, which as I suppose, has been held in Canada several years ago and which will be adapted by your dear father for a confirmation service in his congregation.

I was highly moved in reading it as Anne's words form such an important part of the service and I hope that the young people will be inspired by her message and that her faith, courage and optimism will be meaningful for their future lives.

Forgive me if I do not send a special address, but everything I could say is already contained in the text of the service.

I am sure that this confirmation-service will be a big event for your father's congregation and a memorable day for the youngsters and their families.

We were glad to hear that your plans to visit us have only been postponed, but not given up. We hope you are feeling well and are sending you and Kent our love…

While we were singing "Joy to the World," the Three Dog Night big hit, South Vietnamese troops invaded Laos. How far away that awful was to me, in 1971. In contrast, my world was filled with such happiness. We had this soulful black-and-white-pawed Lab named Buffy (after Buffy Sainte-Marie, of course), whom we considered to be our first child. She was the light of our life. But then new life entered our home in the hills: On April 27 in the early evening, after seventeen hours of hard back labor and every Lamaze trick in the bag—from rolling pins to baseballs— Kent and I welcome our beautiful Robert Ethan Wilson. My mom and dad were there, too, to help us along. We drove precious Ethan home to the sound of TinTin's "Toast and Marmalade for Tea."

October 9, 1971
Dear Cara,

Since the announcement of the birth of your baby boy we did not hear from you.

We did write to you at the time, sending our congratulations, and also sent a music box for the little one. We do not know if it ever arrived.

In July I gave your address to a nephew of mine who visited Los Angeles. He tried to ring you up, but could not reach you. We are worried…

10/16/71
Dear Ones:

Never was I more disappointed by a letter! We never received your music box. I've called the post office and will so some more sleuthing throughout the week to try and locate it, but I'm afraid it got lost in the mail.

We're just sick! I wish I could say something appropriate like, oh, it's the thought that counts. And it is. But, I've still fuming! Of course you would be wondering why the silence after sending us such a beautiful gift. On top of your gift being lost, we've changed our phone number to an unlisted one. So when your nephew called, he got some more silence. That made me more furious. How I would have loved to have him over…

Of course, I could have still written sooner, true, but my life has been totally wrapped around the entire being of one little Ethan. He is a fantastic child. Yes, I am echoing the words every mother says about her child, but I choose to forget that. He is fantastic. And he looks exactly like Kent!

I wish I could say that there's a lot of me in him, but aside for a quick mannerism or two, he is the spitting image of his Dad. Huge blue eyes and tremendous dimples on both cheeks, a little one on his chin. He's all arms and legs (Kent is 6'2" and we are both lanky)—a very big boy who, at six months, is already keeping me going non-stop all day. He loves our dog, Buffy, and the dog loves him. They kiss each other, stare at each other a lot. I could go on and on, but I'll save you from the gushing. I'm in love. He's got the kind of wild, enthusiastic spirit that Kent and I hoped he'd have. Just six months on the earth and he's already a fire of a personality.

I think I told you that we were going to have him the Lamaze method, or a studied form of natural childbirth. Well, we did it. Which makes this little boy even more special to us. Kent was at my side throughout my labor. We had trained six weeks for that day. Panting and blowing through our rehearsed labor. Now I was panting and wheezing and blowing for real. He rubbed my back with a rolling pin, fed me ice chips, timed the contractions, and talked non-stop in my ear. He never let me concentrate on my pain, but made me focus on my breathing the way we were trained and that's how Ethan came into this world. He saw both of us seeing him.

We screamed when the doctor said, "It's a boy!" Oh, how we wanted a boy. I had tried to convince myself that I would in no way be disappointed if it was a girl. But I knew I was lying to myself. And when I saw that he had Kent's dimples, I knew God had really gone overboard this time. He made us very, very happy!

I am still nursing Ethan, which is such a pure wonderful way to get to know your baby. He's eating lots of solid foods as well, but the nursing won't stop until he lets me know he's ready. (No, I won't let that carry on too much longer. I mean, he might not be ready until he's eighteen, but that dedicated a mother I'm not!) I feel like Earth Mother every time I hold him to my breast.

Never have I felt so calm and peaceful as when I am nursing. Kent says he never knew me to have such patience. And it's true. I'm the most impatient person with everything and everybody except Ethan. Anyway, he better enjoy it while he's a baby. Because I know this won't be true once he's old enough to fight his own battles. We are having some pictures developed and will send them to you soon.

Life has been very good to us. Although with a new house and new furniture, lots of paint, repairs, carpeting, etc., etc., etc., we're finding that our budget is a bit tight. We still plan on seeing you people some day as soon as we can relax financially here. We're not giving up on our very special plan: to meet you and talk to you and to take hundreds of pictures and give you lots of hugs and kisses. It's just going to happen!

Just to keep you up to date. As I said before, Kent has been very busy—his work required lots of travel. Most of the time he's producing and directing his commercials three at a time. It's the kind of work that involves him every moment. It's hectic and demanding and frustrating but, once it's going well, it's beautiful. Each big commercial is like a little movie. And it's the kind of pace and challenge that Kent loves…I've found it just a little hard to adjust to the pace he's in. Some days I find it harder than others. Especially since I haven't had much luck getting any freelance writing… this has been my main frustration.

I am so sorry your gift never arrived but Kent and Ethan and I thank you with all our hearts for such a lovely remembrance. We still received your note after Ethan's birth and that really was enough. I hope this is a good and healthy year for you both. I realize that I forgot to wish you a happy birthday, Mr. Frank, so please consider yourself hugged and kissed now.

Thank you again. Much love…

November 20, 1971

Dear Cara,

We were glad to hear from you and I would have answered right away to your lovely letter if I had felt well. But this was not the case lately and I could not attend to my correspondence for some time. Now I am alright again.

We are sorry that our little present did not reach you and so we bought another music-box which we sent air-mail registered. We hope Ethan will like it.

Time flies and now your little darling is already 6 months old. We understand fully your enthusiasm about him. No wonder that he has already now such a strong personality having you and Ken as parents. We are looking forward to receive snapshots of him.

You are describing everything from his birth on so vividly that we have the feeling to be his grand-grand parents.

Nowadays not many mothers are nursing as long as you are doing it, but it is certainly good for the baby and I can tell you that my wife's daughter was nursing her children for 8 months.

There is only one thing, however, which struck us: that you are allowing Buffy to lick the baby. It is nice that he likes the little one so much, but it is unhealthy.

You are writing that little Ethan is keeping you busy all the time. But as soon as he will start walking, he will need still more attention. So we believe that during the next year you will not be able to do much creating writing. But as you have an urge for writing we are sure that later on you will find the time to do so.

It will be of interest to both of you to hear that Peter Nero composed a musical work using as text passages of Anne's Diary. Now Jerome Schnur wants to take this work as a base for a TV production and negotiations are pending. We listened to a tape of the Nero work and we were impressed by it, as we think it could have a great impact on today's youth…

We hope so much that you will be able to realize your plans to come and see us not too far a future. After we have been in correspondence now for 12 years it's high time that we meet personally, and make the acquaintance of Kent and little Ethan…

What a year 1972 was! That was when I saw one of my all-time favorite movies, *Harold and Maude,* to the tune of Cat Stevens' incredible sound track. We were all talking about *The Godfather* and Brando's powerful performance. I remember singing along to Don McLean's "American Pie" and daydreaming to Roberta Flack's exquisite "The First Time Ever I Saw Your Face," and of course, Helen Reddy's "I Am Woman." Well-timed, since the Equal Rights Amendment prohibiting sex discrimination passed the U.S. Congress. But it failed to win ratification by the 1982 deadline! The year also marked the beginning of Nixon's downfall. The Watergate scandal reared its ugly head.

1972 was the year Japan regained control of the island of Okinawa from the United States, and also when Nixon made his historic visit to China. Vietnam was as bloody as ever. Nixon ordered mining of Haiphong and other North Vietnamese ports. But by the year's end, U.S. troops in Vietnam only numbered twenty-four thousand.

I remember my imagination spinning when we sent the Pioneer 10 space probe out into the universe with a plaque attached to it attempting to communicate with intelligent life beyond our solar system. Oh how I prayed we'd hear something…

I worshipped health maven Adelle Davis and was consumed with buying and preparing only the healthiest, purest (and I'm afraid my family remembers it all as the yuckiest!) foods on the planet. I was happily involved in a playgroup—a bunch of Lamaze graduate moms and their babies around Ethan's age. It was the "neighborhood" none of us had.

1/10/72

Dear Mr. and Mrs. Frank:

We received your bright red, round and adorable ladybug musical toy! What a fantastic toy! We are not kidding when we tell you that it is a real, true favorite with Ethan. He loves it. He chews on it, licks it, dangles it about him, and of course, sits in fascination when we pull the string and let it sing to him. It is guaranteed to stop him from crying. And we all thank you for that!

Hope your holiday with your family was as fun as it always is for you. And especially wish you a happy, healthy New Year. We had a wonderful Thanksgiving celebration with my and family and friends here at our home, and just got back from spending the Christmas holiday with Kent's family in Jackson, Missouri. It's always a great deal of fun and, of course, it was more so this year because of Ethan. He was in the spotlight the whole time and loved it. Lord, he's just eight months…and complete mischief in his tremendous blue eyes. He loves everyone. Smiles at complete strangers wherever we take him. Thought you'd appreciate the fact that now he pushes Buffy's face away when the playful dog tries to kiss him. He must have read your letter. I know all parents say and feel this way (or I hope they do!) about their own children but he has made our lives so complete. So rich.

You don't know how close we got to seeing you both this Christmas. True. Kent was going to shoot a commercial in Paris and Munich. He said he wouldn't believe the fact that we might meet! And then it fell through. They're going to shoot the commercial out here instead. I had mixed reactions. I wanted so much to see you but then it would mean leaving Ethan behind with the family—I would have stop nursing him. And honestly, I just wasn't ready yet. Ethan probably could take the weaning better than I could. (He's already drinking out of a cup as well as a bottle, as well as a breast. Variety is the spice of life.) Anyway. Fate kept us a family—now maybe Fate will create that opportunity again.

Please send some pictures of you two. I'm sending some of ours to you. Thank you again, dear ones. Much love…

P.S. Exciting news about the Peter Nero musical about Anne. How's it going? More news please!

March 17, 1972

Thank you so much for your nice, enthusiastic letter. The photos of Ethan you sent us are lovely and his looks fit your description. The more we look at them, the more we are caught by his friendly smile and the mischievous look in his eyes. If he was standing already with eight months he must be a strong and active child. We can imagine that little boy is the center of the whole family.

Watching the progress of a child of this age is a continuous joy for the parents. It is discovering every day a little more of its world and the experiences it is making and the impressions it is getting are important for the development of its personality.

We were very excited to hear that you nearly had the chance to come to Europe and to visit us. But as it should have been around Xmas time, it would have been very difficult to meet, as we passed our holiday in a winter resort where we stayed from December 30—January 6. So we are hoping for another occasion in not too far a future.

You ask about the Peter Nero project. After the contracts had been signed with him and the TV producer we had no further news and probably they are working on the script and the music. They have got 18 months time to decide about the final production. I cannot interfere and just have to wait.

Here everything is fine. After a mild winter spring is in the air and in our garden the daffodils and tulips are already coming out. It is fun to work in the garden.

In February we have been in London for a week to visit the family there. Next week I am going to Amsterdam again. We also had many visitors from abroad and Easter-time we are expecting friends from Holland.

Keep well. We are sending our love to the three of you.

Yours affectionately...

I sent Otto the book *Jonathan Livingston Seagull* for his birthday...

June 29, 1972

Dear Cara,

We were very pleased to hear from you again. Thank you very much for your good wishes for my birthday and the delightful book sent as a birthday present from the 3 of you.

We enjoyed reading it immensely and you are right that re-reading it gives one more and more insight in its philosophy. The bird's strife for perfection and self-fulfillment is described beautifully. It shows that it affords a strong character to live as an individual following one's own ideas. It is fascinating to read how Jonathan after having reached the climax of his capacities, learns that he has the duty to spread his message to his brethren. There is much oriental wisdom in the book…

It was the end of 1972 and I was very pregnant with my second child…

Dear Friends:

Here is another holiday and one we hope is filled with much joy, family and healthy, ebullient spirits. We are thinking of your both so much! We want to share a new joy with you. Going to have another baby this April! Very excited—I'm now six months pregnant and bigger than ever. We'd planned to have our babies this close—I know this year and the next will be hassled, frazzled and diaper deluged but, we are still excited in spite of what everybody is warning us! (After all, what can we do about it anyway!)

Ethan doesn't know a thing about any such shared spotlight. He's a terribly funny, joyously active, curious 19 months old. He never walks—he runs. He has us laughing all the time. We take hikes and walks together—join a group of other mothers and babies twice and week and let the wee ones climb, slide, squeal and romp all morning. He keeps us going!

We wish and pray that we could be together—sitting around our fire-place and talking until the wee hours of the morning. We also want you to know, dears, that once we can work our finances out, we sincerely plan to make some sort of constant contribution to the Anne Frank Foundation…

December 12, 1972
Dear Cara and Ken,

We were delighted to receive your sweet letter and the lovely photos you sent us. The one of both of you must have been taken at a very happy moment at a picnick enjoying being together outdoors and sharing your hobby. There is such a loving look in Cara's eyes, and the heart carved in the tree is a symbol of your harmony.

Your description of Ethan's character and behavior and the funny expression of his face on the snapshot complete each other. We can imagine him as an actor in a play written by his mother and his father!

He must be a great joy to both of you. That he will get a little brother or sister soon, will surely be a surprise for him.

Our opinion is that 2 years difference between children is quite right. Our two older grand-daughters are also only two years apart. Of course we agree that it will be a lt of work and a mother has to give up a lot of her own interests for some time to devote herself entirely to the upbringing of the children. But this time also offers many compensations.

Thank you very much for the very special mobile you sent us. It is standing on the table of our living room and it gives up pleasure to look at it and to think of you. For so many years we are hoping to meet each other, but with the new baby coming this spring, we certainly will have to wait another year or two. Let us hope that we stay in good health (we mean the two of us re: our age.)

Your continued interest in the Foundation gives me great satisfaction and I am sending you by ordinary mail the report 1971 to give you an idea of the work done there.

For the coming holidays we intend to go to the mountains together with our dear ones from England. Wishing the 3 of you a specially happy 1973 we are sending you lots of love…

In 1973-74, I was wearing headbands, pukka-shell necklaces, and American Indian anything. Tattoos were a rage, though I never did that. Feminists were at their zenith, and the play-group women and I had some intense discussions over "I am woman/I am mother" conflicts. I was deeply into earth-motherhood and felt the children were being lost in this passionate race of the sexes. Roe v. Wade shook the nation, invalidating state laws against abortion for women up to six months pregnant. Paul Anka's "You're Having My Baby" nearly caused a feminist war. Though staunchly pro-abortion, I had to admit I thought the song was lovely. I think they sent out a hit woman to snuff me.

The movies then were extreme in every way—from the *Last Tango in Paris* to *American Graffiti*. Pea soup would never the same after *The Exorcist* made its debut. I loved anything Jim Croce sang, and John Denver's *"Sunshine On My Shoulders"* still "makes me happy."

The Vietnam War was coming to an end. The cease-fire agreement finally went into effect, and our last troops were withdrawn from Vietnam. By the end of 1974, most of the last U.S. prisoners of war were released. The U.S. government granted amnesty to those who had evaded the draft during those Vietnam years. Unfortunately, for the returning vets, hell only continued—or got worse.

President Ford pardoned Nixon for the Watergate crimes. And on Yom Kippur—the holiest of Jewish holidays—the Arabs attacked Israel. The Six-Day War. It was a bloody, horrible tragedy that rocked the world.

Yet, in 1973 something wonderful also happened: my beautiful son Jesse Kent Wilson was born. Amazingly, the same song, "Toast and Marmalade for Tea" by Tin Tin, played on the radio once again as we brought our second son home from the hospital. I was joyful.

August 25, 1973
We received your fantastic cradle gym! Thank you again and again! It's not only beautiful to look at, but it's Jesse's favorite thing to play with! It's a delightful as well as a stimulating toy and we love you for thinking of our baby so creatively.

To keep you up-to-date on our roly-poly baby, Jesse: he's a big, cuddly, yummy child. We adore him. He's always smiling and cooing. He's terrifically strong. He's so big that people can never believe he's just barely 4 months old and wearing Ethan's clothes that his big brother wore at one year!

Jesse balances our life with his gentle, kissable spirit. Ethan has been so wonderful with the baby we can't believe how smooth the transition has been—we were worried things would be rockier around here than it is. True, things are crazy. Not a moment of time or quiet to myself. I look away for a minute and Ethan has the garden hose and he's watering our front-room rug—or into the refrigerator breaking eggs all over the dogs—or throwing dog bones down the toilet—things aren't exactly calm around here…But he seems to really like his fat little brother. He's everyday gaining a sense of possessiveness for him—wanting us to be sure to take "Jassee" when we go driving—smiling at or kissing the baby whenever he thinks we're not looking (which is more sincere!) And generally reacting in ways that make us feel he's not all together as shook up about the new little person in our lives as we so anticipated.

Kent is happy with a new job—a new direction in his career. Me—I'm enjoying this frenetic life. I don't know if I told you but after having a wonderful pregnancy—I had an incredible, fabulous birth experience. Just six hours of labor with Kent by my side throughout as he was with Ethan, I was able to push Jesse out without any medication and no forceps—Jesse started coming out so fast that he was almost born without the doctor catching him! He placed our huge infant in my arms and let the baby suckle my breast on the table just minutes after his birth. A very moving experience for Kent and me.

Each day seems to get a little smoother as I learn easier ways to handle two active, demanding little guys. And then I got some freelance writing that could be a sort of sporadically steady job and would help to balance out my life even more.

We think of you often—wishing so much that you could meet and hold and play with our boys. You have been so much a part of our lives—my distant, dear adopted grandparents. Wish that we could be together now… What with the insane state of affairs of the world—at least the American part of it—is in, we find that we have to look for happiness, search for good reasons to be on this choking, festering planet. We have to find hope for our children to build on in spite of the rising inflation, morbid violence, ecological wastelands, Watergate mentality...I just keep buying more plants to fill the house, take walks in the sunshine and groove in the smiles and laughter of my family. And then everything seems like we just might make it after all. Thank you, dear ones, for sharing in our happiness—we hope that you are both healthy and happy and that this year will be a full one for you...

December 7, 1973
Dear Cara,

We were just planning to write to you at the occasion of the approaching holiday season, when this morning we were surprised by your parcel at breakfast-time. We wondered what it would contain, as you always sending us something special. We like the "butterfly on the rock" very much, as it brings in these gloomy winter-days the promise of a new summer to come. Thanks a lot.

We still have to tell you how much we like the snap-shots you sent us some time ago. You and Ken look so happy and well having little Ethan at your side with his cunning look. One can imagine him doing all the mischief you are describing so humorously. You must have good nerves to take it this ways. On the other picture on which you are licking ice-cream you look like a beautiful Gypsy. And baby Jesse is really marvelous, smiling already when he was only one month old. He seems really to be an especially well developed child and far ahead of his age. It is really a blessing that Ethan is not jealous of his little brother and a good sign of his character. As they are so near in age the 2 boys will soon be able to play together.

We were glad to hear that Ken likes his new job and that you have the prospect to do some freelance writing. You surely must have a great talent for writing which shows itself in every one of your letters...

Shortly ago we went to Mannheim, Germany where our nephew lives with his family. He is an actor and we saw him in several plays; among others is "Championship Season" which was also a big success in New York.

As you can imagine we were highly shocked about the unexpected attack of the Arabs on Israel on Yom Kippur and are now mourning all those who lost members of their families. Israel is totally isolated and can only count on the help of the United States which realizes the danger of the Russian imperialism in the Middle-East and so Israel is not only fighting for its existence but also for the freedom of the Western World. Europe however does not think further and is only concerned with the oil-crises…

A small parcel is on the way to you containing a little something with pressed flowers from Israel.

Wishing you, Ken and the boys a wonderful holiday-season and a happy, healthy and successful 1974, we are sending you lots of love…

3-74
Dear friends:

We received your beautiful flower-pressed coasters and we simply oohed and aahed over each fragile one. They are lovely and we thank you so much. Especially since the flowers were from Israel.

Our brother-in-law, Eli, was called back to Israel to help fight during this last war. We were so frightened for him since we knew he was involved in some highly secretive and dangerous work being that he was part of a specialized troop there. Thank God, he's back home now—greatly saddened since so many of his troops—his friends since childhood—were killed. A political war—with the world's oil dangling over the lives of a tiny nation. Israel fights on but I wonder how long they'll be able to do it…Russia is doing everything it can to smother the little country. But, I didn't intend to start out on a sad note, this is 1974 now and let's pray it will be a more peaceful year than last year was.

My family is loving our two boys and our tumultuous home! It always takes me days to get myself going again after the fun and flurry of the holidays. We went back home again to Kent's family in Missouri. It was an enchanting time with snow and sledding and a visit to an old farm and lot of happy, laughing children and adults surrounding us.

And Jesse! That fat little guy. Almost nine months already and he's tremendous and doing everything he can to keep up with his roaring big brother. He's a joy and we're both finding our little boys sooo much fun as they grow into their own distinct personalities.

I do find that there are days I wish I could just close the door and keep walking. But I've surrounded my world with many warm, intelligent women whose hands and heads are as full of children as mine and we find great strength in knowing that we're not alone and that our demanding little tykes will, indeed, grow up some day!

So I am busy. Still doing some freelance writing whenever it comes in and doling more writing on my own now as well as resuming dance lessons. I'm much easier to live with when I've had some time to myself! And Kent is so busy. He's doing some of the most beautiful work he's ever done and enjoying new directing freedom. I'm terribly proud of him. We had so much fun together this holiday I just hate it when he has to go back to work—but that's a reality and I never was good in dealing with it!

'74

My dearest friends:

It has been so long since we've had a good old talk. At least, it's been awhile since I've sat down and answered your lovely, newsy letter

Enclosed in this package is a very much belated birthday gift for you, Mr.Frank—please send us a picture of you wearing it! Happy, Happy Birthday to you (and if you'd come out here, we'd celebrate it with much flourish—balloons, cake and ice cream and many kisses)—can you reveal your age? Also included are the most recent pictures of the boys, we thought you'd enjoy them.

And Jesse is Mr. Peaceful—whereas Ethan is an extremist, Jesse is like a beautiful young redwood tree—strong and resilient and someone who give me a great sense of calm. He is also quite funny. He follows Ethan everywhere—eating anything Ethan hands him—plants, dog food, yogurt, books and papers—Jesse will manage to stuff it all in his always open mouth if Ethan gives his approval. We are joyous in the fact that they, indeed, love each other.

Kent and I are happy and well—knock wood—Kent busier than ever directing commercials and me chasing and rarely catching these crazies that greet our day every 6 am—I also started teaching a movent class to a group of mothers once a week and still write sporadically. All is well, dear ones, and we love you both!

June 7, 1974
Dear Cara,

It is a long time ago since we received your last letter. We had intended to answer it much quicker, but it never came to it somehow…

In April we spent 3 weeks in Israel. By the way we did not know that you have a brother-in-law who is Israeli. As it was our 4th visit to the country we did not do much sight-seeing. Our purpose was to see relatives and friends and to show our solidarity with the people still suffering from the consequences of the Yom-Kippur war. Luckily there were again many tourists, among them numerous Christian groups.

In the meantime the political situation looks like a little brighter thanks to the tireless efforts of your German-Jewish Kissinger. Let us hope that he will give his good services also during the forthcoming negotiations in Geneva.

…We always have great pleasure in reading your letters, as you are describing everything so vividly and humorously. You are certainly a born writer and we are glad that you still find time to do some freelance writing.

We can imagine that you and Ken are observing the growing up of your 2 little boys and are comparing everything Jesse is doing with what Ethan did at the same age. You surely can already judge a difference in their personalities.

It is wonderful that Ken is so satisfied with the work he is doing, but we understand that you are missing him when he is too much absorbed by it.

September 10, 1974
Dear Cara,

It is quite some time since we received your parcel and your last, charming letter. It was so thoughtful of you to send me something for my birthday, even belated. You do not seem to realize that I am an old chap, now 85 years old. As much as I like the T shirt I really can not wear it at my age, but I thank you for your good intention.

We were very pleased with the snap-shots of your 2 boys. They look so healthy, happy and lovely. You are describing their behavior so precisely that we can see them before us.

Ethan seems to have inherited his vitality from you, and though we do not know Kent we imagine that he is a calmer type and Jesse is taking after him. "Opposite characters are attracting each other" is an Old German proverb. This is the case with you and Kent and also with the boys. They must be a permanent joy for both of you.

We can understand that you are reluctant to come to Europe as long as the kids are so young. After all you are writing they have a wonderful free life in your lovely house and garden. It would be difficult to keep them quiet in a hotel. As much as we would like to meet you all, we have to be patient.

CHAPTER 6

A Visit Missed, a Visit Planned—

At Last!

In 1975-77, I was garbed in peasant-style dresses and skirts. Seemed a natural look for me...maybe my Hungarian roots surfacing. The "ethnic" or "layered" look, it was called. I wore baggy everything and funky hats, boots, and headbands. Later, I'd wear ties and vests—very "Annie Hallish." And jeans, jeans, everywhere jeans—my favorite uniform even today.

The biggest deals were skateboarding and that hot dance craze, disco. The Bee Gees were synonymous with that popular move and sound. Their "Jive Talkin'" was a biggie, along with Elton John's "Philadelphia Freedom" and Paul McCartney and Wings' "Silly Love Songs" and "Listen to What the Man Said." The movie industry pumped out some cinematic greats: *The Man Who Would Be King, Close Encounters of the Third Kind,* and *Star Wars.*

The last Americans were evacuated from Vietnam; South Vietnam surrendered to the Communists, and the Middle East battled on.

Meanwhile, I was heavily into my family, two play groups, the L.A. Zoo, and a parent newsletter.

5/75
My dearest friends—

I walked into a bookstore—bumped against a book rack—heard a thump and when I looked down, saw what fell at my ankles: Anne Frank: A Portrait in Courage, by Ernst Schnabel! I bought it immediately, chilled by the strangeness of it all—why that book out of the thousands that filled the store should fall at my feet?! I haven't read it yet, but felt deeply compelled, once again, to talk about Anne with my distant "grandparents," whom I long to meet."I must know more about that great young woman with the Herculean faith in the good and the just of life. Please send me the most recent information on what the Anne Frank Foundation is doing. I would like to feel even somewhat a part of it.

I've been keeping a journal of boy boys since their births—it has given me great joy to record these unfolding, little people—and I feel a sense of immortality about them, too. Somehow you don't completely die when you've left your thoughts behind you. Anne still gives me strength as she did when I first wrote to you over 17 years ago.

I'm now thirty and a part of a hectic home with three other people, two dogs, two birds, two fish and a very fat mouse. I find that time after time I need to dip into Anne's spirit and renew my own spirit.

Today was "baby" Jesse's first day at pre-school! He is now 2 years and 4 months old and Ethan is 4 years and 4 months old. They are wild as ever, but so much fun—so zany—so loving—so TOTAL in their commitment to whatever they're into! I will be glad for my free mornings while they're in school. I plan to continue touring as a docent at the L.A. Zoo and also take a few "animal" classes there and I also hope to continue my writing. I am anxious to balance my life more. I'm a much better person to live with when I am feeling peaceful inside. It's a constant goal of mine. Thankfully, I have Kent to help me out and back me up. He is an incredible father and the boys adore him—as do I…

8/18/75

My dear friends:

You won't believe how close we came to seeing you. I wrestled with the idea of even telling you about it. Kent was going to shoot a commercial in

Switzerland and he said there would be no way he was going to go without me. The whole thing was going to happen last month—he had found out about it on Friday and we were supposed to be in Europe on Monday. I was in total shock. What to do about the children? My passport? MY GOD!!! My head was a mash of worry and euphoria: the children were so young— who would take care of them and the dogs and the plants—when would I have time to get my passport and if I passed this whole thing up, how long would it be before I would embrace you—actually see you, talk to you in person, drink your wine and/or tea—my knees were weak, my spirit was soaring and I finally concluded that the children and all other lovely spirits that made up the jigsaw picture of our home, would, indeed, make it for the eleven or so days we'd be gone.

And then the whole thing fell thru. Kent ended up in Texas instead, and I was full of all kinds of mumble-jumble feelings of relief and despair.

My dearest Otto and Fritzi, we know each other so well and yet don't know each other at all. I can't stand not seeing you. At least, send us another recent picture and after we get ours developed I'll send you some.

I've just finished an article that I hope to see published somewhere— anywhere—so keep your fingers crossed.

My greatest high beside my family has been my joyous feat of becoming a docent (teacher-guide) at the Los Angeles Zoo. I take tours of children once a week to meet the animals I can't seem to live without. I am never as happy as when I am around animals, or reading or writing or talking or learning about them. So after I passed a rigorous four-month course of animal studies at the zoo I have plunged into all the rare and wondrous critters that make up our sorry planet, and once a week at least I can find a solid reason of hope to offer children. If we give up on our animals and our children, we give up on life. I am convinced they are what life is all about.

I know you have been full of anguish about Israel. I share your agony, believe me. It is almost more than we all can bear seeing and hearing what that feisty, beautiful nation has had to endure. And yet, because of their undaunted passion, I have always felt close to my people—the biblical people—the Jews...

Kent and I talk about Israel and the tragic babies of a sick, meaning-less, shameful Vietnamese war—and of the earth's millions that are dying while others roll in fur coats scraped from the backs of endangered animal species.

Our world is imbalanced. How can people die of hunger while others grow fat? The only things that make any sense—and any dignity, purity, reason for living are the children—and the animals and insects and plants that go on living in spite of the predation around them. I hate to think how long they will last, but as long as they can survive this mess, so can I...

September 8, 1975

Dear Cara,

Summer is nearly over and your letter is still unanswered. But as the New Year started we want to send our best wishes to you and your dear ones.

Though we have no young children and dogs around us we are always quite busy, but of course we have not your juvenile energy any more.

It was sweet of you to send us the lovely photos of your boys. The little one changed a lot. He seems to be more placid, whereas Ethan shows a mischievous smile. It is wonderful that they are so near in age that they are company for each other.

What a shame that the occasion offered Ken to come to Europe fell through! We too were quite excited when we read about the possibility to see you both here. But now we really hope that you will be able to spend your holidays in Europe taking the boys along.

It was new to us that you are so fond of animals that you took a course to be a teacher-guide in the Zoo. It will interest you to hear that the Basel Zoo is a very famous one, as it has much success in raising young ones of animals which do not give birth in Zoos in general, f.i. gorillas...

As you can imagine, we are not a little more optimistic about the situation in Israel. We now have to wait if the agreement reached by Mr. Kissinger will really mean a first step to peace and if it will be kept in the right spirit. Otherwise you are right that the world is in a mess and nobody knows the roots of all the aggression, fanatic nationalism and terrorism. Anyhow we do not despair as we are getting from many decent people so many signs of good will, and this gives us strength. All the best to you and your dear ones and lots of love…

Yours affectionately…

November 5, 1975
Dear Cara,

It's time that we are giving you a sign of life again, and to answer your last letter. It really was a strange coincidence that the Schnable book fell to your feet in the book-store. I am very astonished never having mentioned this book to you. In the meantime you will have read it and seen that is a very important book as it tells about what happened before and after we went into hiding and gives a good background of the time of the occupation of Holland. We went to Amsterdam again and have notices that the visits to the house do not diminish, on the contrary there were 25% more visitors than last year.

The work of the Foundation continues steadily subsidized by the Government. It consists of courses for underprivileged groups of the population and seminars for teachers and students of social academics about discrimination and prejudice.

On our way to Amsterdam we stopped in Frankfurt, Germany, to talk to my lawyer on account of an anti-Semitic slander connected with the diary. In a book about Hitler it was called a falsification. I succeeded in the meantime to get a court-order to confiscate the book, and I am asking now that the publisher set the matter right in advertisements.

Apart from this disagreeable affair we also have nice experiences. We were for 2 days in Geneva to meet the choir of the Japanese Christian friends of Israel; with one of its members I am in correspondence for many years. The choir gave a concert there which we attended singing Japanese and Hebrew songs among which was, "A Requiem for Anne," a beautiful piece of music. We invited the group to visit us in our home and all 18 members came over and we had a very enjoyable afternoon together. From here they went on to Israel to give concerts there.

We always like the stories you are telling us about your boys. We are surprised that little Jesse is already going to a pre-school, but we understand very well that the 3 free mornings are very welcome to you, so that you have time for the work connected with animals which is giving you a counter-balance to your duties at home.

It is wonderful to know that you and Ken together with the 2 boys form such an island of love in this unrestful world. We still have hope as the children are now a little older that there will be a possibility to come to Europe so that we finally can meet each other.

All the best and our fondest regards and love to all of you…

Dearest Otto and Fritzi—

We received your delicious box of cookies and loved every delicious last crumb! Thank you so much—we'd never tasted anything like them before and they were a treat for all our family and friends over the holiday season! We had to hide them from the boys and only give them a few each day because they were so crazy about them! Yummy! We loved that picture you sent us—you both looked so strong and healthy—so beautiful against the backdrop of mountain snow, I want so much to be with you people!

We hope you had a lovely time with your grandchildren over the holidays—we want to extend the invitation to any of your family and/or friends that if any of them are out in California they must come and see us…Our home is open to any people you love!

In your picture you looked like you both had been skiing. Are you skiers? Kent and I and both Ethan and Jesse took skiing lessons this holiday—you would have laughed seeing our little boys flying down the little snowy hills in their miniature ski outfits complete with sunglasses! The little guys did a lot better than Kent and I! We had a terrific time and hope to go back soon if our hot California winter will hurry up and get cold! We are having a July experience now! It's the hottest winter since 1923!

April 27, 1976

Dear Cara,

...Now your idea about a telephone-call, I agree with you that it would be great to hear each other's voices and thereby to feel close. But I know by experience that I would get very excited and surely would not find the right words. So I think it is better not to follow up this idea.

Little Jesse seems to have inherited his parents artistic qualities being talented in painting. His cards are really interesting and we like them.

For the summer we have not yet any plans, but a number of visitors announced themselves already. We wish you were among them.

December 1, 1976

Dear Cara,

It was a thrill for me too, to talk to Kent and to feel your loving thoughts through him. What a pity you could not come with him, so that we would have had a chance to meet.

I understand that he felt you near him while visiting the Anne Frank House, knowing your deep involvement for Anne and what she stands for...

Now we are wishing you, Ken and the boys a very happy holiday-season, too, hoping that in 1977 we finally hay have the chance to meet you all. Lots of love to the 4 of you...

January 24, 1977

Dear Cara,

We are glad that the cookies finally arrived and that parents and children enjoyed them. We hope that you also received the little book I sent you which contains a little citation from Anne's diary.

Now I want to thank you for your nice present which arrived safely. We lit the candle when we had my sister and her husband for dinner...

I am quite well again and we went to London for the holiday-season. We had a lovely time with children and grandchildren who were all at home. We saw many friends and relatives who all came to see us, as we did not want to go to town. Our daughter's house is situated in a beautiful district outside of London and we could make nice walks. London was full of tourists who took advantage of the low pound to buy cheaper than at home. Now we intend to go to the mountains for a week as a vacation there does us always a lot of good.

We wonder if your hope to meet each other will be realized this year. We don't give up hope. Will you please thank the boys for their drawing, which show the temperament of each of them. It is most rewarding and exciting to follow their spiritual development and we can imagine that their questions can not always be answered easily.

Our nephew who is an actor in Berlin and his wife will probably come to Los Angeles and visit friends there. If their plan will be realized we shall give them your address. His name is Buddy Elias.

Keep well and happy. We are sending you all our love...

1977

My dearest Fritzi and Otto!

I can barely believe I am about to say what I am about to say but—there is a chance that I may fly out to see you this summer! It's true—Kent and I have talked about nothing else since we started this idea. My dearest Kent wants us to meet NOW and will not allow me to tell him the Reality—that financially I don't know how we can do it, and yet he's convinced me that a few weeks on my own, doing something I've dreamed about for almost 18 years can't be such a crime.

It would only be a few days here and there adding up to about two weeks away from the little family I've never been away from—visiting friends in New York, Holland and YOU! YOU! Where will you be in June—July—August? Would it be best to meet in England? I would want to see the Anne Frank Foundation so very much, and am considering late June or mid-July. Please let me know your plans, because I will meet you wherever you say. I still can't believe these words—I'm dying to go yet so afraid to leave...

Write soon—much love...

June 6, 1977

Dearest Cara,

Your letter containing the exciting news that you may come over this summer only reached us with delay, as we have been in London for about 3 weeks and did not have our mail forwarded. It would be wonderful to be able to meet finally after so many, many years of correspondence.

Now to our plans for the summer. We arranged with our family to meet in a Swiss mountain-resort from July 14th to the end of the month. Otherwise we have no plans to be away from home. So you can arrange your itinerary accordingly. We understand that you also want to go to Amsterdam to visit the Anne Frank House. There is an interesting exhibition in the house: "Ultra Right in Western Europe." You will also see the new statue of Anne which was unveiled in March.

We are looking forward impatiently to hear at which date we can expect you here. We can imagine that it will mean a great adventure for you to travel alone to Europe for the first time, leaving Kent and the little boys at home.

By the way we gave your address and telephone number to a nephew Buddy Elias (son of my sister) who is an actor in Berlin. He intends to make a trip to America with his wife, staying a few days in Los Angeles where they have good friends. This will be sometime in July. He promised to phone you, but if you will be in Europe just then, they will not be able to meet you, but perhaps Ken and the boys. Buddy and his wife are lovely people.

We want this letter to be off and hope to get good news from you soon.

Lots of love to the 4 of you...

Through Otto's coaxing, Buddy and his beautiful wife, "Bambi," arrived at our home. The two were traveling the States from Berlin and spent a brief few hours with me. They were delightful; Buddy had toured the United States for 14 years as a skater in "Holiday on

Ice," and continued in show business as an actor in the movies, on TV and the stage. His lovely wife had been an actor at one time as well. How strange that Buddy should enter my life at that particular time. Somewhere inside, I couldn't help but think that Anne was planning all this, arranging to bring her relatives and friends together.

Over bowls of fresh summer fruit we all talked at once, trying to learn as much about each other as fast as we could. It was a particular joy to meet Buddy, the beloved cousin of Anne Frank. He was very animated, funny, dramatic—bursting with life and vitality. I could easily understand why this vibrant man was an actor. His large, dark eyes sparkled with intelligence and warmth. As I watched him laughing and talking I felt Anne's spirit. I knew that this was how she truly was. I couldn't wait to ask him about her. "Did you know Anne very well?"

Buddy shot back in his sharp German accent, "Of course! She was my cousin! We were very silly together, practically the same age."

Her cousin. I was actually eating cantaloupe with Anne Frank's cousin! "What was she like?"

"A brat!"

"C'mon."

"She was! Also a tease! A practical joker. She wanted to be an ice skater with me, which I was for a while. She would dream of our doing duets on ice together." He laughed, then paused. "She had beautiful, expressive eyes."

6/77

My Dearest Otto and Fritzi—

I am so excited I can barely allow myself to think about the trip too much. It's like dreaming about moon-walking or start-floating: so abstract and unbelievable. I plan to arrive in Zurich from Amsterdam at 11:25 am via SR 791 on July 30th. I am not sure if I will see you at the airport or should I call you when I arrive? Maybe you could leave a message there at the airport or possibly tell Miep, who I definitely will call upon my arrival in Amsterdam (July 27-29—I will probably stay at a youth hostel across from the Anne Frank House.)

I fell in love with Bambi and Buddy and friend, Pat. They are incredible people and we felt as if we already knew each other—the emotion and conversation were overflowing. I wish we hadn't such a brief time together.

I thought I'd let you in on my plans while in Basel. How would you like a behind-the-scenes tour of the Basel Zoo? The director of the zoo here in L.A. has promised to send a letter of introduction for me to the Basel director so I can see this most prestigious zoo. I would love to have us all go together! There is so much I want to talk about with you but must save for LATER! My time in Europe will be fleeting—I leave on August 4, probably from London so we will have to cram our time together in a few, wonderful days.

Hug yourselves for me! Much love and kisses.

June 29, 1977

Dear Cara,

It was wonderful to speak to you on the phone and to get the confirmation that your plans to come to Europe have taken shape.

We are very excited at the prospect to have you here with us, so that we finally shall meet each other personally. As we told you we shall return from our holidays in the mountains on July 28ᵗʰ or 29ᵗʰ and it would be good if you would phone us from Amsterdam the exact date and time of our arrival in Basel…

The best time to call is in the morning between 8 and 9 o'clock or in the evening at about 7. We shall write to Miep about your visit to Amsterdam and ask her to meet you…it would be nice if she could meet you at the Anne Frank House and show you around. We shall mention this idea when we are writing her.

As my wife told you on the phone we shall make reservations for you here in Birsfelden, (Hotel Alpha) as soon as we know the exact date of your arrival. We want this letter to go off quickly, as we soon will have the occasion to speak about everything personally.

Looking forward very much to your visit we are sending lots of love to you and your dear ones…

CHAPTER 7

A Dream Realized

July 15, 1977

Dear Cara,

We just received your letter and hurry to answer you. You are asking if we would meet you at the airport, but this is not possible and would be too complicated for us. We advise you to take the Swiss-Airbus to the terminal which is at the railway-station and take the next train to Basel, which will take about one hour and a quarter.

If you could manage to ring us up from the terminal, this would be the best to do, so that we could meet you at the Basel station.

We do not know who gave you the idea that there is a youth hostel next to the Anne Frank House. This was the case years ago. But of course there are youth hostels in the city.

We were glad to hear, but not astonished that you like Bambi and Buddy. So do we, otherwise we would not have asked them to get in touch with you.

It was a good idea to ask for an introduction to the Basel Zoo and of course we shall love to go there together.

Just as you are looking forward with great excitement and expectations to meet each other finally, we appreciate it greatly that you are undertaking this trip to Europe mainly to visit us and...we are extremely happy that you can carry out this plan at last and are grateful to Ken that he agreed.

We are wishing you a good flight and hardly can wait to have you with us.

Lots of love…

That was my last letter from Otto before my trip to see him after almost twenty years of correspondence. Otto was eighty-eight and Kent kept encouraging me to "…meet Otto now, before it's too late."

I was terrified—this was the first time in my life I was journeying by myself. Up to that point I had never been anywhere alone. Frightening thought. But with my husband's insistence, and his family in Missouri generously caring for my two little boys, I tearfully embraced them all in a fierce first-time-ever good-bye hug. Ethan clung to me a little longer—a few tears mingling with his infectious smile, then my little ones, ages five and seven, disappeared into a cluster of relatives.

Suddenly I was alone in a strange, summer-hot airport, sipping chamomile tea and re-reading Anne's riveting words made so famous in her Diary, while flies buzzed me from nose to toes and my tea got cold. I had never felt so alone. What in the world had I done? What if Otto wasn't anything like I pictured him to be? What if he just shook my hand and we had a very reserved discussion over some more tea in some strange Swiss restaurant and then I was expected to leave? But where would I go? My family was thousands of miles away…and just when I was about to call the whole thing off, my Boston connection was announced.

And so my journey began. From California to Missouri to Boston to London to Amsterdam on a plane as big as a building, carrying East Indians, Italians, British, Americans, and others. It was like a symphony of global accents volleying from aisle-to-aisle. I semi-slept all night listening to the wails and whines of other people's children and slowly found myself a tad guilty enjoying this temporary aloneness being just me in my own bones, with nobody calling me "Mommy" for the first time in years. I continued reading the Diary, wrote in my journal and pondered my trip again.

As Buddy and Bambi had orchestrated it, my pilgrimage to Otto would start in Amsterdam, meeting Miep and Jan. Anne mentioned the incredible Miep many times in her writing—she was Otto's loyal secretary, the non-Jew who was one of the key lifelines for the Jews in hiding in the annex above Otto's spice factory. There were three other office workers who worked alongside Miep and were also entrusted by Otto and the others in hiding. They were Johannes Kleiman, Victor Kugler, and Bep Voskuijl—each very courageous and selfless individuals.

Miep had sought out sympathetic friends, also non-Jews, who would set aside extra food, clothes, books, etc., for her without ever asking why they were needed. She and Jan, her husband, had just been married when the Franks were forced to go into hiding. The tension and anxiety they all went through would prevent Miep and Jan from being able to conceive; and it would be more than five years after the war before their only child, Paul, was born to the middle-aged couple.

Buddy's words still echoed in my mind. "You, of course, remember Miep from Anne's Diary. We'll write to her and prepare her for your visit. She'll show you around the Anne Frank House herself, so you can see it through her eyes."

The Amsterdam airport was glistening wet, looking like a mysterious film noir movie. To add to the drama, one piece of luggage was lost for awhile. As I waited for it to be found, I, too, felt lost and alone.

A taxi ride later I was in front of the neat little brick apartment building where Miep and Jan lived. She opened the door to their tiny apartment and shook hands with me. She was a strong, short woman, sixty-nine years old then, with light-blond hair and a direct, no-nonsense air...a lovely Viennese savior who had reluctantly become a famous hero.

"Hello, I am Miep. And this..." she turned to the tall, lanky, white-haired Dutchman, "...is Jan." In the Diary, Anne had referred to Jan as "Henk," one of a great many names, Miep explained later, that had been changed for their protection.

The couple shyly and in a halting mix of English, Dutch, and German arranged to meet me the next day at the Anne Frank House. After much discussion over my plans, I left to check in at the small hotel where I would spend two nights alone; a long nap was just what I needed now.

The next day the cab driver dropped me off at Prinsengracht 263. I stood outside the tall, narrow brick building and stared. Bicycles sped by. Tourists snapped away. Houseboats bobbed gently along the canal. I stood like a statue in front of the looming specter that had once housed and hidden Anne Frank. A click and a buzz of the door, a long steep climb up endless stairs into the main office. People everywhere. Leaflets, books, and glass-encased articles and newspaper clippings—examples of racism and universal persecution. A guest book fat with the signatures of people from around the globe. I looked out from the ceiling-high front windows down to the cobblestone street below.

"I'm sitting cozily in the main office, looking outside through a slit in the curtain. It is dusk but still just light enough to write you. It is a very queer sight, as I watch the people walk by; it looks just as if they are all in a terrible hurry and nearly trip over their toes. With cyclists, now, one simply can't keep pace with their speed. I can't even see what sort of person is riding on the machine." –Anne Frank, *The Diary*

An elderly couple in matching beige raincoats stood waiting below. I tapped on the glass and waved. They looked up and waved back and entered the building. Miep, once again, was in the Frank House.

"Will this be painful for you, Miep?"

She put her arm in mine briskly, and I took up her stride. "No, Cara, I have been here many times, though it hasn't been for a while. I have yet to meet the new director. No, I am really fine."

The students behind the counter shook hands with the couple. They had recognized Miep and were genuinely pleased to see her. Jan was always by her side and his calm demeanor seemed to balance this volatile lady with the fire still burning in her eyes. As she talked to me, her voice carried above the hum of the crowd.

Little clusters of the curious began trailing us. Those who had not recognized her asked, "Who is this woman?" "How does she know so much about this place?"

I wondered if perhaps Miep was pleased that she was becoming a focal point. There was a bit of the performer in her—she always had a dramatic flair when she spoke, but you couldn't ever doubt her truthfulness. She commanded my immediate trust and attention and I doubled my steps to keep pace with her, as the tour got under way.

"This," she said, circling one room, "...used to be my office. I sat right here; Bep *("Elli", in the Diary)* was over there; and Mr. Kleiman *("Mr. Koophuis", in the Diary)* next to her. Over there is where Mr. Kugler *("Mr. Kraler", in the Diary)* and Mr. Van Pels *("Mr. Van Daan", in the Diary)* worked." It was like a scene from Our Town.

We walked up some more steep stairs to another creaking landing. I tried to ignore the flashbulbs popping around me, the ticket takers, the crush of people—always too many people when I most wanted to be alone. I focused on the past, and everyone else didn't matter.

Miep pulled me on. "We cannot use those wooden steps anymore. Not safe." She pointed to a covered grating at our feet. "But those were the original steps we took to get from the office to here." We walked through a narrow passageway leading from an unobtrusive-looking gray door that doubled as a bookshelf. Up another steep stairway and we were there. Inside "the secret annex."

I took a deep breath, hoping to inhale some history. It smelled too clean. Miep pointed to a freshly painted wall. "This used to be their closet, right here." She bent over the miniature model of the annex and described it the way she remembered so vividly.

"Here is where Anne would write her diary...right here by the window, in the room where we stand. I remember once taking a picture of her as she was writing. She looked up at me, slammed her book shut, and stormed out of the room. She was very angry with me for doing that. Yes, she had a temper.

"But she also loved to laugh and talk all the time, too. When I would enter the room after giving my special knock, they would all be standing silent, expectant, fearful, excited to see me, to hear what I had to say. No one would say a thing, except, of course, Anne. She would rush up to me and immediately what to know, 'Well, Miep, what's the news? What's happening?' She was a lovely child, very fragile-looking, with large, expressive eyes."

"Sometimes I believe that God wants to try me, both now and later on; I must become good through my own efforts, without examples and without good advice. Then later on I shall be all the stronger. Who besides me will ever read these letters?" *Anne Frank, The Diary*

We walked from one tiny area to the room where Anne had slept near the washbasin and tiny W.C.; she slept in the same room as Mr. Pfeffer (*Mr. Dussel, in the Diary*), the dentist, whom she disliked. Then up another flight of creaky stairs to the Van Daan's quarters and the communal kitchen.

"This is where they would listen to the radio," Miep said. Jan nodded. "Yes, I would spend many hours visiting with them all listening to the radio together right here."

"There was a cupboard here. And this table here is where they all sat and ate." Miep pointed around the room: Anne would sit here. Mrs. Frank here. Margot here. No, no, no...Peter would sit here and Margot there. Mr. Pfeffer...was he here? No, right here. Mr. and Mrs. Van Pels over there and there.

"And it was right here," she pointed so dramatically and with such passion that a chill shot through me and visually impacted the little group of people who followed us in hushed silence clinging to her words, "...right here is where I found the Diary."

"I stared at the place on the floor, hoping some vestigial aura would still be there. Miep and Bep had entered the upstairs annex after the Nazis had taken its occupants away. When Miep discovered the piles of papers and books strewn all over the floor she recognized the writings and the red-checked Diary as that belonging to Anne. Immediately, they gathered everything quickly and placed them in Miep's desk until the time when she hoped the family would be released and she would hand it all back to Anne.

"I never read a word on those papers, nor her diary, and it was a blessing that I didn't," Miep said, "Because had I read Anne's manuscripts that were her diary and her stories, I would most assuredly have burned them all. She had mentioned too many names. She was actually in the process of changing our names—(hence, Miep Gies became *Miep van Santen*; Jan Gies became *Henk van Santen*; Bep Voskuijl became *Elli Vossen*; the Van Pels family became the *Van Daan family*; Fritz Pfeffer became *Albert Dussel*; Johannes Kleiman became *Mr. Koophuis*; Victor Kugler became *Mr. Kraler*.) A lot of people's lives would have been greatly endangered. Yes , it was fate I didn't read those papers…"

The tourists could contain themselves no longer. The questions burst through the air. Who was she? Miep answered them all, and turning to each cluster of followers she would exclaim, "Did you read *The Diary*? Well, I am Miep of *The Diary* and…" she proudly pointed to her shy Jan, "…this is "Henk!" The place went crazy. Everyone crowded around her, asking for autographs, grabbing her hands, taking her picture, smiling through misty eyes, staring in disbelief. Miep, of The Diary was actually standing in front of them. If it weren't for Miep saving Anne's words there never would be *The Diary of Anne Frank* at all.

As Miep and Jan talked to the crowd I walked into the next little room. Peter's room. He was the beautiful teenage boy who I fell in love with right along with Anne. Peter was such a sweet and handsome adolescent who once studied, brooded, fumed, daydreamed, cried and loved in this very room. He was the subject of many romantic passages in Anne's Diary.

An ancient wooden step led from Peter's room to a small entryway in the ceiling. It was roped off at the top so one could only climb up and peer into the darkness…the attic where Anne would spend many hours alone writing, staring out the window, lounging in the small patches of sunlight filtering down, catching the feel of fresh air and a glimpse of the passing seasons. The world outside.

"The sun is shining, the sky is a deep blue, there is a lovely breeze And I'm longing—so longing—for everything. To talk, for freedom, for friends, to be alone. And I do so long…to cry! I feel as if I'm going to burst, and I know that it would get better with crying; but I can't, I'm restless, I go from one room to the other, breathe through the crack of a closed window, feel my heart beating, as if it is saying, "Can't you satisfy my longings at last?" "I believe that it's spring within me, I feel that spring is awakening, I feel it is my whole body and soul. It is an effort to behave normally, I feel utterly confused, don't know what to read, what to write, what to do, I only know that I am longing…"—Anne Frank, *The Diary*

Later, Peter would join her and they would hold each other. I loved the fact that we couldn't enter this special sanctuary. I imagined that the balls of dust and lacy cobwebs held some of the past. It smelled old and damp. Perfect.

I walked back to the entrance where Miep and Jan continued signing autographs and posing for pictures. The director, Cornelis Sujik, wanted to meet them for a chat and some tea. Would they come to his office, please? I joined them for awhile, enjoying the theatricality of their animated conversation in Dutch. After a time I excused myself, explaining I'd return a little later. I wanted to see a bit of Amsterdam, the canals, the street that Anne was so desperate to be a part of. As I walked, I began feeling very Dutch myself, loving the sound of my feet on the worn cobblestone—and the sad, faraway chime of Anne's Westertoren clock.

"Daddy, Mommy, and Margot can't get used to the sound of the Westertoren clock yet, which tells us the time every quarter of an hour. I can. I loved it from the start, and especially in the night it's like a faithful friend."-Anne Frank, *The Diary*

Miep and Jan were just coming out of the building. She swept her arm into mine and once

again I was taking two steps to her one to keep up with her. We hopped in a cab; its windshield wipers beat like a metronome in cadence to our conversation. I asked Miep a question.

"How is it, Miep, that when the Dutch or Green Police came for the Jews that you, too, weren't captured? After all, you were an obvious accomplice."

She smiled conspiratorially and tapped my arm. "Oh, that is quite a story. I will tell you when we are home." This was definitely going to be good. After jumping out of the cab (was there anything slow about this lady?) we practically skipped to their little apartment. Finally, warm and dry, we sat in the immaculate front room. Doilies and lovely European artifacts, prints on the wall, a loudly ticking clock. Miep settled into the couch to tell the story.

"The day it happened I was at my desk in the main office, two floors above the spice factory, one floor above most of the office workers. I remember the door being opened and five men entered the room. One was wearing a Nazi uniform; the others were in civilian clothes, and probably Dutch Nazis. The five seemed to know everything, and the German officer came over to Mr. Kraler, the office manager, and said, "Take us upstairs. We know the Jews are here. His eyes seemed to look through us. He knew. Someone had told them.

"Upstairs, near the bookcase, the five drew revolvers, opened the secret door and went inside, climbing into the annex. Then they started pounding away, tearing down books, ripping everything apart. The families reacted quietly, as if in a trance. They put some of their clothes into bags without talking.

"When the officer found Otto's German military footlocker and realized this Jew had once been an important German officer in World War I, the Nazi was really shocked. He almost saluted. He kept saying over and over again, "Don't rush. Take your time. Take your time." But all eight of them including, including Otto, were herded downstairs at gunpoint, toward a waiting van. I was standing behind my desk. He pointed the barrel of the gun straight at me. I will never forget that feeling.

"Now it is your turn," he said. I stared back at him. You see, I had recognized his accent. He wasn't Dutch, but rather, Viennese, like myself.

"With the gun still pointed at my face, I answered, `But you're from Vienna. So am I.' Well, the man went crazy. After all, here was this woman who was from his homeland. It shocked him, and he started pacing the room like a caged animal, shouting at me.

"`Shame on you for hiding Jews'...I said nothing. `What am I going to do with you! What do you think I should do with you?' I still said nothing...just stared back at him.

"Finally, he came over to me. `Alright. I will not do anything right now. You will continue to work here and you must not ever leave town. I will come back and check on you and make sure you are here. If you dare leave, I will take away your man.'"

Miep winced in pain remembering it all. She practically whispered the words, "Then I said a stupid thing: `He knows nothing! My husband knows nothing!' But, thank God, the officer didn't question me anymore. He did come and check on me many times but never said anything. Just made sure I was there."

"Countless friends and acquaintances have gone to a terrible fate. Evening after evening the green and gray army lorries trundle past. The Germans ring at every front door to inquire if there are any Jews living in the house. If there are, then the while family has to go at once.

If they didn't find any, they go on to the next house. No one has a chance of evading them unless one goes into hiding. Often they go around with lists, and only ring when they know they can get a good haul. Sometimes they let them off for cash—so much per head. It seems like the slave hunts of olden times. But it's certainly no joke; it's much too tragic for that. In the evenings when it's dark, I often see rows of good, innocent people accompanied by crying children, walking on and on, in charge of a couple of these chaps, bullied and knocked about until they almost drop. No one is spared—old people, babies, expectant mothers, the sick—each and all join in the march of death." –Anne Frank, *The Diary*

The clock in the room ticked louder. Miep excused herself to prepare dinner, and Jan and I talked about their son, Paul. The tall, reserved Dutchman mellowed when he talked about his child. The silver and china glistened as we sat for dinner; the formal setting was very natural to them, so very European and correct. I found myself missing my grandmother—the fiery Hungarian lady, Gizella, whose own apartment and table and general style were not unlike that of Miep's. How many times had I sat at Grandma's perfect table just like this…

Miep's story wasn't finished. She told me how she and Jan still didn't give up; they went to the baker and the grocer and many other brave Dutch people to ask for money to try to bribe the Nazis into releasing the Franks and Van Daans and Dussel. There had been cases where such bribes did work, so Miep gathered the money together, went straight to Gestapo headquarters, walked right up to the same portly officer who had pointed the gun at her face and without saying a word, rubbed her thumb against her fingers in the universal symbol meaning "money."

The Nazi shook his head. "It won't work anymore. Too late. They are already gone. Anyway it won't work." The good old days of excess were dwindling because Hitler's regime was weakening.

Miep stared back at him. "I don't believe you." The Nazi pointed upstairs. "Go and talk to my superiors if you don't believe me. But I tell you it won't work anymore." So she charged up the stairs and opened the door.

Sitting around a table was a group of Nazis intently listening to an English radio broadcast. They sat very straight when they saw her and screamed, "Get out! Get out!" She turned and walked down the stairs past the Viennese officer. He said, "I told you so." She kept walking and closed the door behind her—and with it, hope for her friends.

Our dinner was finished. Miep and Jan cleared the table and insisted, as a guest, I must not help. Then they reappeared, carrying dishes of deliciously cool yogurt with fresh summer fruit.

The conversation continued. I was curious about Otto—and very anxious to see him. I knew he was the sole survivor of the band of Jews from the annex. Where did he go once he got back from the concentration camp?

"He came to us...to Jan and me. He was deeply depressed. Very, very nervous. But he had lots of friends to visit and offer his help. He was constantly working to reunite displaced concentration camp victims with their friends and families.

"He always found someone who needed support. He also was very involved in Anne's Diary. It took him months to read all of it. It was terribly painful for him," Miep said. "He stayed with us for seven years doing his work, but we didn't really see that much of him because he was busy every minute and even returned to work in the spice factory below the annex.

"Fritzi was also in his life. They dated for the seven years Otto lived with us, and it brought joy to them; they finally were married. It was an interesting story as to how they first met on a train coming back from the concentration camp. Fritzi's husband and son had died there, but she and her daughter, Eva, had survived; Eva had been a friend of Anne's. So Eva introduced her mother to Otto, because their parents had never met.

"Life was happier for Otto because of her and they took great pleasure in our baby, Paul. They loved him very much. You will love Otto. He is a wonderful man."

The talk of Otto made me restless. It was growing darker and I would have to leave very early in the morning to catch a train for Switzerland, my ultimate destination. Miep and Jan put on their matching raincoats and took my arm to accompany me on the tram back to my hotel. I felt so close to these two incredible people. On the tram, I turned to Miep and held her hand tightly, and told her how proud I was to know her. I said that women, especially, must know her story—must learn of her courage. It would inspire them. They would share my pride in a woman who never gave up fighting. Miep shook her head; she wanted no praise.

"Cara, what else could I do? Anybody would have done the same. You just do what you have to do. That's all."

The tram stopped at my hotel. My new friends embraced me. I looked into their faces with such love. I could feel Anne's presence and understood why she loved them so much. I never wanted to forget these war heroes. I gave them another hug, and they were gone.

I stood for a moment in the lobby, trying to gain some perspective, feeling terribly heavy and serious inside. I hadn't really laughed or been silly for much too long, so I paused to talk to the young people working behind the desk. One girl had a craving for a special kind of Lindt chocolate bar and I wanted some magazines with lots of pictures and no heavy reading. I told her I would try to find her candy if she would just point me in the right direction.

I found my spirits lifting and my youth returning as I walked the twilight streets of downtown Amsterdam. Young people, their long-hair flowing laughed and talked, lovers embraced, curbside musicians and scraggly students mingled with those privileged by wealth and beauty—a street tapestry weaving around me, lifting me back to the present. I felt lighter until the butterflies returned to my stomach.

Tomorrow I would meet Otto Frank.

CHAPTER 8
OTTO: Infinite Signs

In the morning, at the train depot, I lugged two huge, heavy suitcases full of too many clothes that I had been warned would be unnecessary to take with me. Obviously, I didn't listen and didn't know how and what to pack, because I carried half of my entire closet with me. I was supposed to be in third class, but was too exhausted to drag all that luggage through car after car, so I collapsed in a pool of sweat in a corner near a window. Since all the seats in the car were filled I sat on my bulging suitcases and listened to bits of animated conversation in French, Dutch, and German. I watched the rush of scenery speed by—a monastery, a glimpse of the Rhine appearing here and there as a blink of a bridge spanned from one bank to the other. Church spires pushed through clumps of forest. Barges hauled their weighty cargoes through the dark water.

I leaned my head against the cool window glass as the rhythmic clacking lulled me into a dreamy state. I thought of trains and how the Holocaust death trains took the victims to the camps while others returned the survivors to their shattered—or non-existent—homes. But this train was gratefully different. This train was taking me to one of the most famous survivors in the world—the father of Anne Frank. A man I had adored for years.

I imagined how it was going to be when Otto and I met for the first time. Of course I wanted it to be all emotion, embraces, tears. But that was my script. That was "Scene A"—the way I wished it would be. Life—as I was constantly learning—usually didn't conform to the dramatic scenes in my head. "Scene B" was more the backup plan—not the one I wished for, but more realistically probably the way it would all transpire. No, Otto would probably shake my hand quite formally, a little shyly, and we would have a very civilized time together—brief and cordial—and then, a busy man, Otto would have to go to his next appointment. I hated that scenario, but I was prepared.

Then I heard it. The conductor distinctly said, "Basel!" There. He announced it again. This wasn't a dream. I stood up and rubbed my numb behind, which felt as though it had the entire indentation of suitcase handles and tags. The postcard backdrops outside my window had suddenly disappeared and Basel Station screeched into view.

Doors flew open and a tide of pushing, shoving people carried me outside like a giant wave. I staggered into the middle of a buzzing swarm of humanity, hundreds of passengers trying to get out and in at the same time. A handsome young German took pity on me as I struggled with my impossible luggage and practically lifted me onto the platform.

Scanning the crowd I saw her immediately. Fritzi looked exactly like her pictures. In an instant I was hugging this tall, striking-looking woman. In her strong German accent she exclaimed, "Cara, I thought you were shorter from your pictures next to Kent!"

"Oh, I am, Fritzi—it's just the sandals. They add a lot of inches!"

"Where's your luggage?"

"Right over there—oh don't try to pick them up. They're far too heavy, believe me! Where's Otto?"

"Over there, see him? He is looking for you."

Oh God. He was right over there. That beautiful man with the straight back and Lincolnesque face. Chiseled features. High, carved cheekbones and snow-white hair around a balding head, his skin a patchwork of dark and light pigmentation. A very tall, elderly gentleman—statesman-like, strong and handsome and formally dressed. He was wearing a crisp white shirt and tie under a black overcoat. It was really him. Otto Frank.

He turned to me. Smiling. Arms outstretched. "Cara! At last!!!" And just like that I was actually being hugged by Otto Frank. A real bear hug! Thank God! Goodbye "Scene B!" No formal handshakes. No polite hellos. This was IT—"Scene A" all the way! We pulled away and stared at each other. Suddenly a little shy, Otto put his arm in mine and Fritzi linked my other arm as we walked off into the sunset, the music swelling as the credits rolled. No, Cara, no, no, no! This was not a movie, a dream, not even a daydream. This was the real, unscripted way I prayed it would be.

I snuggled close to by precious bookends and found myself scrunched into a taxi and then swooshed out in front of my new "home" in Basel—the Hotel Alpha, a beautiful relic from long ago. My room was as tiny as it was crisp and immaculate—like a miniature thirties-era dollhouse, complete with a little box of Swiss chocolates on the desk at the foot of my bed. A gift from Fritzi and Otto.

"Do you like it, Cara?"

I loved it, but I was ready to take the tram to their street. It was just a short run. I could easily walk to their house; that's why they had picked that hotel. Their home was so small, they told me, and it was uncomfortable to have guests in such close quarters. They hoped I understood. I did, and was very happy with my private retreat down the street.

As we walked, linked arm-in-arm, I looked up at the street sign. There it was, the name I had written on so many, many envelopes through the years, and it pointed to the most immaculate, silent, beautiful old street I'd ever walked on. The homes, three-storied and square-shaped, were elegantly subdued in their austerity, each surrounded by walls and hedges. We pushed open the iron gate leading to the Franks' home and Otto unlocked the front door while I took in the aroma of rain-fresh flora. Fritzi said the people living upstairs did all the gardening; the Franks preferred this duplex arrangement because the neighbors cared for the Franks' home in their many absences.

We went inside and walked up wooden stairs to a platform where another door awaited unlocking. The smells of age and coats and a basement somewhere and heated air brought back a childhood memory—a hotel lobby kind of smell. Now it was Fritzi's turn to unlock and slide open this second door in a routine that seemed to be understood and part of their comfortable ritual.

Their home was filled with rich, dark colors—lots of earthy browns and maroons and pillows and little sculptures, prints, books and bright doilies. Under every object there was a delicate lace doily, white filigree amid the browns.

Fritzi opened up a cabinet and picked out two objects—a paperweight and a sculpture. She saw I didn't recognize them. "You've forgotten? These are what you sent us many years ago. We keep them here."

I hadn't remembered them at first; they'd been sent so very long ago by a long-ago me. I was touched that they had saved them all these years. While Fritzi disappeared into the kitchen, Otto took my arm and ushered me outside to a little covered patio and a couch with table and chairs among sweet peas and potted plants, a cozy place without fencing, an entry into the backyard where there were more plants, trees, and a tangled vine of shiny blackberries. Otto searched to find the plumpest ones to pick and hand to me. We ate blackberries together.

I took a deep breath and embraced the fresh flower scent surrounding us. Then Otto showed me the source of such sweet aroma. Roses. Everywhere roses. And over there, he said, the most special rose of all— the fragile orange and pink, "Anne Frank Rose," created by an admirer in Anne's memory.

Fritzi reappeared with a wooden tray filled with a lunch spread. And then they took me into their little study where the two answered the volumes of daily correspondence. A pile of fresh, as yet unopened, mail lay stacked on Otto's desk; correspondence from all over the world. Otto said, "...here is where we answer them all, Fritzi and me!"

I took in a quick panorama of this sacred inner sanctum—two typewriters in two corners of the room, a few pictures, prints on the wall and a sketch of Anne. Another chest filled with mementos from friends and travels. Family photos and a plump pillow tucked into the couch with the names of Anne Frank Club members embroidered in all colors decorating both sides. Fritzi said it had been made by a young Danish girl, Mette, who later married and had a daughter she named Anne. It was beginning to be more and more obvious to me that Otto's "family" was bigger than I had ever imagined. And soon he confirmed that fact.

Opening a large cupboard, Otto pointed to shelves of ceiling-to-floor notebooks literally bursting with letters from people all over the world. Seeing my eyes widen in awe, he nodded, "Cara, you are not the only one to write me all these years. There are many, many like you."

Of course. Why should I be the only one to adopt Otto? I was intrigued. Who were the others? Fritzi and Otto smiled as the names and faces of this uniquely international "family" came to mind.

There was Sumi, from Japan, who had lost her father when she was just three years old. Her mother put the child in a nunnery, where she was converted to Catholicism. As a young girl, Sumi read Anne's Diary and was moved to write to Otto. She told him since he had lost his two daughters and she had lost a father, she asked if she could become his "letter-daughter"—and signed all her letters, "your daughter, Sumi." Otto advised her through the years, as he did me and she, too, appreciated his wisdom and advice. Once she graduated from college as an English major Sumi looked for work and responded to an ad from Twentieth Century-Fox requesting a secretary fluent in the English language. Sumi gathered all her correspondence from Otto and, accompanied by a nun, introduced herself. The corporation, impressed by Sumi's longstanding relationship with the father of Anne Frank, gave the young woman the prestigious position. Otto and Fritzi had already met the lovely Japanese woman and showed me a picture of the three of them smiling together.

There was the young man, Ryan, from Carmel, California. He'd had a lonely life with his mother living a meager existence. He was a dropout from school—a dropout from everywhere—a true lost soul. When his mother died she left him their tiny house and Ryan was completely alone. And then someone gave him Anne's *Diary of a Young Girl* to read.

Ryan had been a boy with no intellectual life; not a reader, his only real talent was his ability to draw. He sketched everything. After reading the book he told Otto and Fritzi in his first letter to them that his life had changed. This young girl, Anne Frank, reached him, talked to him, had given him something he'd never had before—hope. He became obsessed. He had to meet Otto and he had to go to Amsterdam and see the Anne Frank House.

He sold his house and with around seven thousand dollars, left immediately for Amsterdam. Once there, he begged the director of the Anne Frank House for a job; he not only wanted to work in the House, he wanted to live there. When he was refused because he wasn't a Dutch citizen and because living in the House was an impossibility, the desperate young man stayed nearby as long as his money held out. Ryan started to sketch everything—people, the canals, the countryside. And, of course, the Anne Frank House. I saw his beautiful works in both Miep's and the Frank's homes—his artwork looked like fine old prints. Ryan was extremely close to the Franks—they considered him like an adopted son. His personal story about his connection with them is truly quite moving and is now being shared in his remarkable book, *"We Never Said Goodbye."* Eventually, Ryan became an extremely successful illustrator working for a large publishing firm in the States. He continues giving talks about Anne Frank and Otto to schools and organizations everywhere. Ryan remained very close to Miep until her passing and has become a very dear friend, like a brother of mine through the years. He is equally very close to Eva Schloss, Fritzi's daughter.

Then there was Barbara, a devout Jew who had been writing to "Uncle Otto" and "Aunt Fritzi" for many years as well. She brought her husband to meet the Franks on her honeymoon. Barbara now lives in New York with her family and lectures on Anne Frank to school groups and Jewish organizations and more. Otto and Fritzi were quite proud of Barbara because, "...she is spreading Anne's spirit."

The Franks had been corresponding with many Russian young people, but found the frustrations of censorship too great; many times the letters would never reach their destination. Otto no longer wrote to them because he couldn't maintain an honest communication.

John Neiman was a college student in 1974. That's when he read *The Diary of Anne Frank* and became so inspired that he wrote to Otto. Two years later, John flew to Switzerland and met Otto and Fritzi in person. A deep friendship began and John became a close friend to the Franks and Miep and Jan as well. Then in 1979, John had a profound discussion with Otto in London. Otto said something life-transforming to the young man who had been so moved by Anne's story; his words would change the entire course of John's life. The elderly man advised, "If you really want to honor Anne's memory and the people that died, you do what Anne wanted so very much to do—do good for other people."

For John, a devout Catholic convert, that meant becoming a priest. Otto Frank had spent the remainder of his life after the war always being of service to others—and John Neiman decided to follow Otto's example. Six years after Otto's death, John became a priest and Miep and Jan flew to Los Angeles for Father John's ordination. Father John became a cherished friend of mine (and my entire family as well!) whom I consider to be a beloved brother to this day. I, too, attended that most memorable occasion when he was ordained a priest. Today, Father John, a priest now living in West Virginia continues to reach out to a huge network of Holocaust survivors, schools and organizations lecturing frequently on every aspect of Anne and her family and the Holocaust. He remained in close contact with Fritzi and Miep until their deaths years later.

And then there was that wonderful girl, Vassa. An incredible story. In the mid-1950s, Otto had received a letter written in Greek from a young girl from Athens. In order to understand the letter Otto went to the Greek embassy where he was referred to a local Greek teacher who translated that letter and subsequent letters for him. This young girl, Vassa, told Otto about her horrifying background. Her father had been in killed in the underground movement when Greece had been occupied by Germany. His death left Vassa, her brothers and sisters and mother alone and ultimately homeless. Deeply depressed, the young girl lost interest in everything—in her studies, in life itself. Then one day she read in the paper that the play, *The Diary of Anne Frank*, was to be performed at the local theater. Even though she'd never heard or read about Anne before, Vassa was intrigued by the play's description—the sad life and ultimate death of this beautiful young person in the Holocaust. After seeing the play, Vassa read Anne's book, and then wrote to Otto. And as we all seemed to do, Vassa poured out her heart to this faraway father figure—Otto Frank. His response to Vassa reinforced the fact that though Anne was deprived of see her goals achieve, dying as young as she did, Vassa had a whole lifetime of hope and promise ahead of her. Their correspondence continued for several months, and with Otto's constant encouragement, Vassa overcame her depression and finished her studies at school. Realizing that she no longer needed his advice, Otto wrote to her explaining that it was too much strain having to translate her letters; he said he was getting too old and had limited time with his demanding schedule.

For over a year Otto didn't hear from the girl; then a letter came signed with her familiar signature. The letter was in French—a language that Otto could speak and read quite fluently. During those months Vassa had studied the French language so that she could continue corresponding with her mentor, Otto Frank.

Later, she became a French high school teacher, married, and had two children—a boy, and a girl named Anne. Otto and Fritzi once visited the family in Vassa's Athens home.

There were so many more fascinating stories of "Otto's children," too numerous to recount here. The young Yugoslavian girl, Ljuba, whose boyfriend became so jealous of her correspondence with Otto that he threatened to kill her! Fortunately, she married another man, much to Fritzi's and Otto's great relief.

And there was Teti—the second Greek girl to adopt Otto. She, too, wrote Otto in French after reading Anne's Diary. Teti told Otto how her parents reproached her for being a factory worker. Apparently the parents had far more respect for Teti's sister, who worked for a radio station. Otto answered that no work is insignificant if you do it well, but he also encouraged her to try to "get a more important job." She did just that and soon was chosen to represent her company at a fair in Munich, pleasing her greatly.

One stormy evening at ten o'clock, the Franks' door bell rang. Opening the door, they found a young girl standing there drenched and shivering. Teeth chattering, she whispered, "I am Teti."

After they gave her warm clothes and a hot meal, Teti told them that she didn't want to go home. Could she stay with the Franks and try to find some work in Basel? She was welcome to stay, and Otto promptly said he'd try to help her, but it wouldn't be easy since she spoke no German.

Again, he went to the Greek consulate, asking for the address of local Greek citizens and soon found the perfect situation for Teti—a Greek family with two children, who were eager to have her live with them and help with their French and English homework lessons.

When Teti wrote to her parents about her new teacher/au pair position, they were quite impressed. The young Greek girl stayed with the Basel family for more than half a year, visiting Otto and Fritzi often. She learned German and even dated Otto's nephew, Stephen.

Finally, she returned home, and gratefully found her parents now receiving her with new respect. Teti married an officer—a man she had known long before she left Greece—and had a son. The Franks visited Teti and her family in Athens, and the correspondence continued even after Teti's husband (many years older than she) had died.

The Franks little office was brimming with notebooks filled with so many letters—endlessly compelling stories like these. "I received most of my letters from America. But can you guess from which country I received almost as many letters?" I rattled off a few guesses, all of them wrong. Otto's eyes twinkled. There was still mischief within him. He answered me in his sort of German-British voice. (He would say "half" and "can't" like an Englishman.) "Most of the young people we hear from," he said, "...are Japanese."

The Japanese people identified with Anne's persecution and related her Holocaust experience to the horrors and repercussions of atomic warfare in their own past. Otto told of the Japanese Christian youth group he met in Israel. They were observing some ruins there and Otto came over to them, introducing himself as the father of Anne Frank. When they heard this they started shouting and crying and putting gifts in his hands and hugging him.

As he recounted this story, Otto's eyes filled and he took out his handkerchief and blew his nose. It was the only time I would see him break down. He felt these young people were an extension of Anne. It was the joy in the present that brought tears to this sweet man, not the bitterness of the past.

He was like a father/grandfather to us all.

In time, that entire Japanese Christian youth group that Otto and Fritzi had connected with so profoundly in Israel later found its way to Basel and the Frank's little home. All the members crowded into the same small room where the three of us sat now. One of the young men in the group became a Christian minister. Reverend Makato Otsuka created the first Holocaust Museum in Hiroshima, Japan; he says meeting Otto and Fritzi in Israel in 1971 totally "changed my life."

I felt so close to all these people. I knew they were but a small part of Otto's extended universal family, and now I have this great desire to meet my other "brothers" and "sisters" around the world. We are from all different races and religions, but in one way we are the same. After all, were we not sent by Anne to keep her father company?

Throughout the weekend we would dine at Fritzi's beautiful table and eat the delicious vegetarian meals she went out of her way to prepare for me, knowing my proclivity for non-meat meals. We would talk, eat, talk some more, and then I would walk back to my little hotel while Otto would nap.

I love the memory of my first night there. I hugged them both good night and, borrowing their umbrella, walked back alone through the little town of Birsfelden, next to Basel. A warm summer rain pounded around me; the streets were glossy and crowded with weekend tourists huddled under awnings or dashing about finding temporary respite from the rain . An accordion squeezed a distant melody from somewhere inside a cozy little restaurant.

I wrung myself out inside the tiny hotel and began writing in my journal and postcards home—"My first Saturday in Basel, Switzerland. Today, I met Otto Frank."

In the morning we had to get in a lot of good talking before Otto's nap, because afterward we were going to the Basel Zoo. The director of the Los Angeles Zoo, Dr. Warren Thomas, had sent a letter of introduction for me, enabling us to get a behind-the-scenes tour of one of the world's most exquisite zoos. I was a docent at the L.A. Zoo and would become a part-time animal keeper upon my return from Europe.

The morning was going fast and there was so much more I wanted to know. We talked about Anne, looked through the family album that Anne had put together, her neat lettering captioning each photo—Margot powdering Anne's bottom, cousin Buddy and Anne as children, more family pictures. And then there was one picture of some beautiful blond-haired moppets playing together in a backyard. They had posed during a brief interval in their game of hide-and-seek, still scruffy with curls aflutter and cheeks flushed. Even in the black and white snapshot they seemed to glow, smiling shyly at their intruder—cherubic little boys at play.

"You see these children, Cara?" Otto ran his finger across each face. "These were my playmates when I was a boy. And they all became—except that one right there—that all became Nazis."

I was riveted. It was hard to believe. No. Not those sweet babies. I wanted to freeze time, hold my hand over their faces and yell at them to not grow up. But they did. They grew up to kill other babies and mothers and fathers. The reality—Nazis were once babies, too.

I sat back in my chair as my eyes traveled from the photo album to the tablecloth, from the fruit and cheese to Fritzi's arm in repose in front of her. Dark, purple-black numbers were tattooed deep into the elderly woman's flesh. She caught my stare. "Yes, Cara, these are from the concentration camp. See Otto's?"

Fritzi's voice broke the silence. "I had been in hiding, too, Cara, with my husband and son and daughter." She brought over a small oil painting, the work of her son before he and his father were taken away. She never saw either of them again. Fritzi and her daughter, Eva, were in the camps together and survived by caring for each other, by being alive for each other. After the humiliation of being shaved from head to pubis, and living like sub-humans, they made it to freedom together.

Through brimming eyes, Fritzi recalled the first moment she met Otto. They had been on the same cattle train from the camps, and as they poured out onto the platform her daughter pointed excitedly to the gaunt man standing alone. "Look, Mama! There is the father of the girl I used to play with down the street! Anne Frank!"

They had lived across the way from each other for years and Fritzi and Otto had never even met—only their daughters had been friends. From that moment, the two saw each other constantly; they courted for seven years. But Fritzi didn't want to leave Amsterdam until her daughter married. After being assured by her future son-in-low that he would never take her daughter to faraway Israel, Fritzi had to relinquish her hold on the child who was life itself to her. Only then did she marry Otto and left with him for Basel—and a new life.

The daughter, Eva, once a successful antiques dealer living in England with her husband (who has since died); they have three daughters, and grandchildren now, and they are all a constant source of joy to the elder Franks, a renewal of hope for Otto as well as Fritzi. In time, Eva would publish extraordinary books about her life and also contribute to a highly successful and deeply moving play. Today, she is in demand worldwide for book signings and keynote talks. Vibrant even in her nineties, her mind is incredibly sharp as is her amazing stamina. She is quite remarkable.

It was time for Otto's nap. Before I went back to the hotel he brought out a huge notebook and placed it in front of me. "Read this, Cara. These are your letters to me—I saved them all." I couldn't believe it. I still can't to this day. Otto had preserved nearly twenty years of my life. I scanned through the tremendous pile of correspondence and literally watched myself "grow up" before my eyes—page-after-page. From large, handwritten scrawl evolving into more adult script, and then onto countless typewritten pages all peppered with masses of ex-clamation points and under linings—outpourings of feelings I didn't remember expressing until that moment. I was facing myself through these letters. Otto had saved—and ultimately validated—my youth in more ways than one…

The rest of the day was a dream come true for me, but I'm afraid it was a rather exhausting one for Otto. He was too old and fragile at that point to go "on safari," touring the Basel Zoo, so Fritzi and I left him sitting happily, protected from the warm summer rain, catching his breath under a shelter. Strong and spry Fritzi seemed to enjoy her-self at the wonderful zoo as much as I did. We were met by Dr. Studer, the gentle Assistant Director, who took us behind-the-scenes of that world-famous wildlife compound. Fritzi and I were treated to an amaz-ing close-up celebration of monitor lizards, antelopes, giraffes, okapis, bongos, apes of all shapes, and infant twin pygmy hippos who sucked our thumbs. I was in animal heaven…what a glorious day! A combina-tion of two of my great loves in one afternoon—with Otto and Fritzi Frank, and being with animals. Never tell me dreams can't come true!

That evening some of the Franks' friends and family stopped by. I met Otto's diminutive, adorable "little" sister, Leni (in her eighties), a tiny bundle of nerves and wit, still very pretty, the mother of Buddy. Full of energy, always in motion, she was still a prosperous antiques dealer, as she had been most of her life. This peppery little lady was yet another extension of her feisty, brilliant niece. As I watched Leni I began seeing and understanding the many-faceted teenager's roots as well.

The group of people who gathered into the Frank's cozy front room was all in their late sixties, seventies, and early eighties; I had never met senior citizens like them before. They were dynamic, teasing, vivacious, very much filled with energy and self-esteem. They spoke in rapid German, hands wildly gesticulating, stopping only to briefly translate for me. The gist of their conversation between talk of vacations and theater and mutual friends was their fury over the new generation of Germans.

The group spoke of a growing, terrifying neo-Nazi movement. It was teaching this new generation that the concentration camps and six million dead Jews were all Jewish propaganda—it never happened, these neo-Nazis claimed. The movement professed that Hitler was a redeemer—a great German leader—and anything that challenged his revered reputation was simply a lie; and Anne's *The Diary of a Young Girl* was the greatest lie of all—pure fiction. I was sick. It couldn't be true what these people were telling me. They must be exaggerating; yet something inside told me that they weren't. Such insane and cruel thinking lived on...

Our last day together is etched so clearly in my memory. We sat outside on the little patio. The smell of flowers filled the air—sweet peas and morning dew and the Anne Frank roses.

Otto opened the door and sat down next to me. He had brought out a whole pile of notebooks and a small, red-and-white checked diary. I gasped.

"This is not the real diary, Cara, it is a duplicate—an exact replica of the original. The real one is in the bank in a safe; but this one is put together exactly like Anne's. I have taped everything little paper just the way she did. We had to be frugal with paper, you know, so Anne wrote on any scrap she could get her hands on."

I turned each page slowly, examined the graceful Dutch script, and saw how she changed her signature after many passages. She had been experimenting—"Anna M. Frank," "A.M. Frank," "Anna Marie

Frank." There was a sketch of a skating dress that she had envisioned herself wearing when she and cousin Buddy would skate their duet. I noticed there was also much writing along the borders of the pages. Otto told me that they were Anne's observations about what she had written before, such as: "I do not feel this way now, but I did then so I won't change it."

> "When I look over my diary today, 1 ½ years on, I cannot believe that I was ever such an innocent young thing…I still understand those moods, those remarks about Margot, Mummy and Daddy so well that I might have written them yesterday, but I no longer understand how I could write so freely about other things." Anne Frank, *The Diary*

And then Otto told me something that amazes me still—Anne had actually rewritten her diary. She had a sort of premonition that her words could very well live on after her. This idea came to her after listening to the daily radio program in which the Dutch minister, Bolkestein, had said how fascinating it would be to someday gather all the diaries and letters of all the Jews in hiding after the war and discover what their lives had been like. That hit a note with the young writer.

> "…my greatest wish is to become a journalist someday and later on a famous writer. Whether these leanings towards greatness (or insanity?) will ever materialize remains to be seen, but I certainly have the subjects in mind. In any case, I want to publish a book entitled Het Achterhuis (The Secret Annex— literally: "the house behind" translated from Dutch) after the war. Whether I shall succeed or not, I cannot say, but my diary will be a great help…" Anne Frank, *The Diary*

So she began editing her diary, refining her writing. Otto emphasized that she never changed the message of each passage, but would only perfect the writing so it would read better. Anne Frank was truly a brilliant writer in every sense of the word.

Along with her almost daily entries, she had also rewritten her earlier observations into four packed notebooks. The original diary is written to not only "Dear Kitty" (both a friend's name and a character in a favorite book) but to others friends as well. The rewritten diary sticks to only Kitty. Anne also stopped experimenting with various sign-offs and decided upon a simple, "Yours, Anne," because she wanted continuity and no confusion—just a flow of thought. She even censored herself, thinking that some passages would be entirely too boring. Otto put many of those extracted passages right back into the published Diary, particularly those dealing with her love for Peter. He felt that young people would greatly identify with this kind of pain called "growing up." Anything too intimate he left out.

I looked at the thick notebooks and my awe magnified for this vibrant spirit, this very old-beyond-her-years teen. Within that tiny, sequestered apartment she wrote and rewrote one of the greatest works of literature in history. She was keeping herself alive. And she was a liberated woman decades before any of us were.

> "I want to get on; I can't imagine that I would have to lead the same sort of life as Mummy and Mrs. Van Daan and all the women who do their work and are then forgotten. I must have something besides a husband and children, something that I can devote myself to! I want to go on living even after my death! And therefore I am grateful to God for giving me this gift, this possibility of developing myself and of writing, or expressing all that is in myself know Anne." Anne Frank, *The Diary*

(Note: Today, the unabridged Diary is available to the public under the title, *The Diary of Anne Frank: The Critical Edition.*)

"Otto," I asked, "did you know that Anne was so creative, so sensitive?" The question saddened him.

"I did not know that side of Anne because she never let any of us know that side of her. I would have expected her sister, Margot, to have such depth of emotion, but Anne...she was so temperamental, so private, so very funny. No, Cara, I did not know my child."

The Gemini teenager would write:

"I've already told you before that I have, as it were, a dual personality. One half embodies my exuberant cheerfulness, making fun of everything, my high- spiritedness, and above all the way I take everything lightly. This includes not taking offense at a flirtation, a kiss, an embrace, a dirty joke. This side is usually lying in wait and pushes away the other which is much better, deeper and purer. You must realize that no one knows Anne's better side and that's why most people find me so insufferable." Anne Frank, *The Diary*

It took Otto months and months of time and draining emotion to get through the writings of his dead daughter. When he had compiled a completed manuscript, he sent a copy to his mother. Other people read the work and finally Otto was urged by many others to let it be published. The world must know about Anne Frank.

I looked at the old man thumbing through the pages of the little checked diary (which represents only a fragment of Anne's writings.) How very much like her father Anne must have been. She seemed to have resembled him physically as well. The slightly protruding front teeth, the shy smile, the handsome, striking features, the quick sense of humor, the sparkling, penetrating eyes, the keen intelligence. Anne Frank's father was looking through her Diary and I took a picture so I would never forget.

Later, while Otto napped and Fritzi cleaned her kitchen, I gathered Anne's short stories around me and read a few of them before I fell into a dreamy sleep on the patio. I had never felt her presence so strongly. It was a growing moment for me. I realized I was not Anne Frank reincarnated as I think I secretly wanted to believe years ago. I was not Anne at all. Wasn't brilliant like her. My fate wasn't her fate. There was a whole world of loving family and friends and adventures still waiting for me back home. I was glad to be me—to be in this moment of time.

Being so close to Anne's ink impressions and next to the man she so lovingly called her "Pim," helped me to focus my attention forward. I couldn't resurrect Anne. I couldn't adopt Otto. But I could keep their message of love and hope and alive. That I could do.

At the tram station I turned to Fritzi. Otto was resting across the room. "Fritzi, does it bother you that people react so strongly to Otto? So many times, because of Anne, he is the focus of attention. Do you ever feel upstaged?"

Fritzi looked so poignant, so earnest. Her face softened into a glow—this strong, kind, elegant woman whose face has known so much more sorrow than laughter.

"Oh no, Cara. My whole life is for Otto. I love to help him, work along with him. There is nothing I want to do more in all the world."

I hugged her. I knew it was this woman who had helped Otto to live again, not only by helping him answer the incredible letters pouring in from around the world, but more—she had helped him feel joy in her presence amid the constant reminders of their tragedies.

I looked at my darling Otto sitting so straight and serious. I wanted to remember every word he spoke, every touch…how he stroked my hair, patted my hand, and said over and over again as we briefly toured the ancient streets of Basel, "We can't see everything, Cara; just a little, just a little."

And I would always remember his face as he told me quietly, "It was good that you came now, Cara. I'm a very old man, you know."

The last time I saw him I was staring back from inside the tram. As it pulled out of the station he was standing so tall on the platform, his strong, sweet lady by his side. She waved in my direction, and he clasped his hands together and swayed ever so slightly toward me—a Jew at prayer. And I saw there were tears in his eyes, too.

CHAPTER 9

Epilogue: Changes

Our letters continued for three more years until August of 1980, when Otto Frank died. Fritzi wrote me:

Dearest Cara,

Now my darling Otto has left me and all his friends in the world. Though I know that he wanted to die after his long and fulfilled life with the many sad but also happy events, I miss him terribly. I am glad however that you still saw him when he was his own lovable self. Luckily he did not suffer and passed away peacefully...

This book was one of the hardest challenges I've had to face. For all my efforts are living in the *now*, and everything in this work is in the *then*, where I truly didn't want to go.

It is a book of reminders, of ghosts—of a house in the hills, a marriage, a cozy, secure world that is no longer but has been replaced by an entirely happy, yet completely different scenario. Change, I have come to understand, is an integral part of life. My sons, Ethan and Jesse, are now grown men with wives and children of their own (Jesse with Branda, son Nicholas and step daughter Autumn; and Ethan with Fabiane and son, Kaio.) I am now "Nana"—a name that suits my soul completely. And though my marriage with Kent ended years ago, we still are good friends, as I am with his lovely wife, Rosana; and my wonderful husband, Peter (my "Peach"), and his grown son, my step son Adam and his wife Faina, are now the added elements to a family that have still remained close in spite of the changes.

Change, as this book reflects, is keenly apparent in every moment—every decade. It seems I've had to say goodbye to so many—including in time farewells to my dear friends Fritzi, Miep, Jan, Buddy, and beloved Otto. Life truly is about letting go—nothing remains the same ever, does it? I'm sure you find that in your life as well.

This book has forced me to watch myself grow up. An over-exuberant, ever-dramatic child. And, as Anne expressed in her diary, I felt a lot of ways then that I don't feel now. Or at least I have gained another perspective. Though the extremism and hatred rampant within the world we live in now reflects much of that time and place in which I poured out my heart to Otto, I now understand to the depths of my being that Love is the only solution to every fearful situation. I believe this with all my heart.

I also didn't change Otto's charming syntax, nor his proclivity for calling Kent "Ken." I left in my own heady sentences, hopes and dreams, humor and pain; and the hailstorm of explanation points!!!!! I read those long-ago letters and see a different me—a "Cara-then" as opposed to a "Cara-now." But how are we different? How are we the same? How did this man whom I so revered truly affect my life? Why did I choose him to have so much power and influence over my life?

Otto Frank obviously fulfilled a need in my life to be validated.

The words "validation" and "choice" are those that resonate with me strongly when I think about what I've learned most of all through that beautiful correspondence and friendship.

If we all took the time to validate each other's thoughts, words, feelings, privacy, even eccentricities what a more caring world this would be, don't you think? To react not in judgment or criticism but with love and compassion is the kindest way to connect with one another.

Otto validated me by not only writing back through the years, but by making me always feel that I mattered to him. He did this for young people worldwide. We all felt we truly mattered to this wise and wonderful mentor. Otto cared for us all and he listened. What a gift. When I discovered that he actually saved my words, all of my letters—like he did for his other global "family"—that was the ultimate validation of his caring nature. I still am greatly moved by this.

Otto encouraged my love of writing, as he encouraged me to be a mother and to really be with and know my children. Many times he expressed his pain in realizing that with all the time and attention he gave to Anne he really didn't know her. The Diary's contents were a shock to him in many ways. He would have thought that his gentle daughter, Margot, would have penned such sensitive missives, not Anne. "Know your children, Cara…" I remembered those words. I kept journals for many years about my sons. The books are treasured and have become a source of great entertainment not only by Ethan and Jesse but now their own families. My grandson, Kaio, falls into gleeful paroxysms of laughter when I read to him what his daddy and uncle did and said as children. And my sons love knowing more about who they are and always were from the start. I am so grateful to Otto for reinforcing the importance of listening to the childhood voices—such a beautiful way to validate their uniqueness and impact on our lives.

Miep validated Anne by respecting her privacy and not reading one word of the young girl's writings. Miep simply tucked them away for Anne until she hopefully returned from the concentration camps. Even when Otto returned from Auschwitz Miep chose not to tell Otto about the saved Diary and the other writing material of Anne's. They were not for him they were for Anne. Only after they received word that Anne had died in Bergen-Belsen along with her sister, Margot, did Miep then give all of Anne's writings to the devastated father. Miep's choice to validate Anne ultimately gave the world *The Diary of Anne Frank.*

Validation and Choices. We do have choices every moment. It might not feel that way but we do. "It's not the load that breaks you down…it's the way you carry it." We all have burdens of our own but we also have choices as to how to deal with them. We can blame others, succumb to the pain, or become bitter, angry, implode. Otto Frank didn't do any of that and in choosing a more positive and loving perspective, he not only helped himself live and love, he helped a whole world of others too. He kept his daughter's spirit and words alive for generations. He read her words and he listened with his heart and he did as she so passionately wished—

"I want to go on living even after my death." –Anne Frank, *The Diary*

Even in Auschwitz Otto chose not to focus on the horror surrounding him, but rather he told a young man that they must envision other things—talks of literature and music and even, he requested of the young man, "…to call me 'Papa', for that is who I am…" Otto was a father and it was his deep love for his two daughters and the desire to reunite with them after they were hopefully liberated that kept him alive. His love for them and his identity of being a father was a choice of love over hate.

"Out of suffering have emerged the strongest souls; the most massive characters are seared with scars." –Kahlil Gibran

There is a revolutionary book entitled, *The Hidden Messages in Water*, by the renowned scientist, Dr. Masaru Emoto. What Dr. Emoto reveals in his astounding work is that even the tiniest of molecules of water are affected by our thoughts, words, and feelings. He shows us how molecules can actually thrive and flourish from good energy or wither from negative energy. It is an amazing book, a true treasure that I highly recommend everyone read to help realize how important our positive thoughts are in not only changing our own lives, but, indeed the entire world. This is how Otto Frank helped changed the world. He chose love over hate—hope over hopelessness.

Otto Frank also taught me another tremendous lesson when I asked him if he knew who betrayed them. He simply said, "It doesn't matter." And he was right. Some things just don't matter. His children were dead, nothing that Otto could say would bring them back. He said later to others, "We cannot change what happened any more. The only thing we can do is to learn from the past and to realize what discrimination and persecution of innocent people means. I believe that it's everyone's responsibility to fight prejudice."

I remember once giving a talk to a group of middle school students about Otto and was speaking about the power of forgiveness. At one point a young boy raised his hand and asked me if I then had forgiven Hitler for what he did to the Jews. The question was like a sucker-punch. I had to think about my answer and then said, "Actually, no I don't forgive him. But I have let him go. I don't want to carry around hate inside me. I have released the weight of Hitler-hate from my molecules."

Some things you just have to release. So even though the idea of forgiveness is powerful and edifying, I find that most of us can accept even more the concept of "letting go" in order to go on with our own lives. At least it works for me—and that young student seemed to agree as well.

Fritzi said about Otto, "Although he believed that Hitler's crimes against the Jews should never be forgotten, he also felt that there was no way forward with hatred."

I am reminded of one of my favorite sayings, *"Holding onto hatred and resentment and anger is like taking poison and hoping it kills the other person."* Every time I feel myself carrying around the weight of negative feelings towards someone else I think of this. And also: *"Before you embark on a journey of revenge dig two graves."* –Confucius

Another lesson I learned looking back on my long correspondence with Otto was that it's a good thing to follow impulse and write to anyone we choose. We don't have to expect any answers back either. It's just taking that leap of faith and showing up to someone we feel compelled to talk to—either through a letter or an email or Facebook or Twitter.

Unfortunately, this new generation barely knows about putting pen to paper, sending out stamped and sealed letters into the world and then waiting, waiting, waiting for the mail to come and with it a response of some kind. Lost is the joy of writing with a solid pen onto crisp paper stock, or even tapping away on a typewriter and feeling like you are truly birthing something special with each ding-click-zip signaling sentence endings and new beginnings...Ah well.

I just want to encourage everyone to connect with whomever they always wished to talk to—be it presidents, authors, kings, queens, wildlife leaders, race car drivers, athletes, adventurers, survivors, scientists, performers, on and on. Who do you admire? Why not tell them? Okay, you might not get an answer back from them personally, but you will feel proud of yourself for simply having the courage to act on your dream. If you hear back, well that's frosting on the cake. If you don't, then pat yourself on the back and admire your "cake" of courage to write the letter in the first place and send it out. Never give up. If I had stopped at the point that Otto told me he couldn't write any more, then I would have lost decades of a friendship that changed my life. I was prepared to just keep writing to him because I wanted to talk to him. I needed to do that—and he understood. No one is too great or unobtainable to speak to.

So, although much has changed in my life and in the world itself since my dear Otto and I corresponded, what has never changed is my love for him and my ever-growing respect and awe for the lessons I continue to learn because of him. Otto Frank took my hand and walked me from childhood to adulthood, as he did for young people all over this world. In our loneliest, angriest, most futile times this grandfather-of-all—this amazing Holocaust survivor—embraced us and loved us unconditionally.

I feel his presence all the time and have come to expect a call to speak about the book oftentimes when my spirit is at low tide. His voice, "Just tell the story" is alive within me, as is his constant belief in the power of forever being hopeful. In fact, ever since my journey continued after Otto died small encouraging signs have buoyed my spirits. Ironically, they've appeared as the number eight. The sign of infinity, it shows up on a torn card at my feet, a seat assignment on a theater ticket, eight friends gathered together spontaneously (I was recently the eighth speaker at an authors' event), or on a bus, truck or cab directly in front of me, on and on and on. Sometime ago I was informed of news that literally took my breath away. "Otto" in the Italian language means "eight." Every time I see an eight I know it is Otto telling me not to give up.

Otto Frank helped me—as he helped his entire global family—believe in planting new hopes when the old ones withered and died. I continue to plant new and ever more positive perspectives every day. Otto would be happy…

CHAPTER 10

Shared Lessons from Otto

"It Doesn't Matter"

Though it's believed that Otto Frank might have either known, or had an idea of who the betrayer was who turned them in on that dark day of August 4, 1944, by the time I had met him at the end of his life—three years before his passing in 1980—it seems he had come to a place of inner peace.

Yes, the sorrow and pain were still reflected in his beautiful eyes, but though he passionately tried to find out in every way who had betrayed and caused the death of his loved ones as soon as he was liberated from Auschwitz in 1945, he finally arrived at a place of inner acceptance by the time I asked him if he knew who betrayed him.

His answer to me was shocking. Quietly, he turned and looked at me saying, "It doesn't matter."

Those words have resonated with me forever. I couldn't understand it at the time but now I do with all my heart. Because there comes a time when we must let go of all the unfairness, the angst, the injustices, indeed, all the rage that broil inside our souls and finally hand them off. Let them go. Move on. If there is nothing we can possibly do to right the wrong, then we must release it.

I say it over and over again, repeating the familiar expression, *"Holding on to hatred and revenge is like taking poison and hoping it kills the other person."*

So how do we focus on what really matters in our own lives? It's so simple. We honor what is before us. Any of the Senses we have right now—Seeing, Hearing, Smelling, Tasting, Touching. And we cherish them. We listen and breathe deeply and savor and embrace—the delight of children and animals and all things natural and wild and untamed; the scent of the seasons and the pavement after a rainfall; our lover's touch and kiss; sunrises and sunsets; stars ablaze in the sky; the constant dance of clouds; a symphony; the joy of laughter, singing, dancing; a child's whispered secret; weeds bursting through improbable cracks; the wonder of seeds awakening, gardens bursting with abundance, the beauty of trees.

What is most significant ultimately is the core of life itself. Love. Once we let go of all that pain tucked inside us, we not only uplift our own lives, but magically, the lives of others as well. When we save ourselves, we save others. Amazing how that works. And that's exactly what Otto Frank did in choosing love over hate. He rescued us.

We have a choice: to hold onto and ultimately fester and die with our fury, or let it go and live the blessings before us while we are still here to celebrate them. That's what matters.

"Just Tell the Story"

Before every talk I give to others I hear Otto's voice inside my soul. What I hear are his words to me, "Just Tell the Story." In other words, this is not about me at all. That's his reminder to me to step outside of my ego. Leave myself outside the door. Be the channel, not the personality to the story about to be told. So whether I'm speaking about Otto Frank, Anne Frank, the Holocaust, the beauty of nature, or any and all kinds of stuff I love to share, none of it is about me. It's all about THE STORY.

I cannot emphasize this enough to all of you having those panic attacks and stage fright before you stand before an audience and speak. If you remember to "Just tell the story" and see yourself as not you but rather a storyteller who has a gift to share with others, I swear there is a perspective that you instantly are given that awakens you. Seriously, re-member, the audience isn't there because of you—unless you're famous in some way. They are there to learn about the topic you are presenting to them. You are the megaphone. The channel. They are the children who love to hear a good story, not to watch the speaker or care a whit what he or she is wearing or looks like.

The story cannot live without the storyteller. You are there to give and share your gift of a story that needs to be told. Get out of yourself and just tell it!

"Write to Anyone"

I cannot encourage you enough. Is there someone you would love to write to but just thinking about the possibility is terrifying? Do it any-way! Please, for me. Just do it!!! You see, I believe that no matter how rich or famous or powerful, etc. a person happens to be—from kings and queens and athletes and Hollywood stars and scientists and astro-nauts-- all the biggest luminaries on the entire planet, here's a secret.

They all have belly buttons and red blood and hearts that beat and lungs that breathe. Just like you. Are they superhuman? Not at all. They're just famous. And they're human.

So if you have this burning desire to reach out and write to them—to anyone on Earth, I pray that you do it. Okay, your letter or email or Instagram or, etc., may never get to them in person possibly screened by their handlers, but here's the thing. It doesn't matter. Because you know what does? The fact that you had the courage to connect with them and show up and tell them whatever it is you wanted to tell them. If you receive an actual letter or note back from them personally then hallelujah! But you may not. And still it doesn't matter. All that matters is that you showed up for *you*!

When I originally expressed the wish to write to Otto Frank I was discouraged by a few family and friends. They said he would never answer me. My letter would never reach him. I'm wasting time. But I didn't listen to any of them. Thank heavens I didn't.

And when Otto wrote in his very first letter to me that he wouldn't be able to continue corresponding because of his busy schedule, even that didn't discourage me. I told him that it was alright and that I just wanted to write to him. And I did. And so he began writing back realizing that I wasn't going away. (Sometimes it does work to be a pest!)

So please reach out and write. You might be genuinely surprised how moved you make others feel that you care enough to want to connect with them. Nobody is superior to anybody. We may be luckier or unluckier than each other, but not better. We are all ONE on this Earth School. We each have our own missions to accomplish that not only change the trajectory of our lives, but that of others impacted by the ripple effect of who we are. We are all students and teachers of each other. Right? Write!

"The Art of Validation"

One of the most stunning moments that still stand out in my memory being with Otto, was him showing me the huge amounts of boxes filled with letters from his global correspondents. From ceiling to floor, shelf upon shelf, the evidence of his universal pen pals had me speechless. I knew he wrote to worldwide youth in particular but I wasn't prepared for witnessing the enormity of his letter-writers. He made me feel so singularly special, giving me the time and attention that I longed for as he did for every single one of us. This was Validation 101.

And then he slipped a huge box off the shelf and set it down in front of me. "These are your letters," he said with a gentle smile. My letters. That wonderful man had saved all the letters, cards and notes I had written to him for over eighteen years time. I was blown-away. Some of those letters are republished in this book but many I've left out simply because I wanted to focus more on Otto and his words and not mine.

But what struck me the most was that it wasn't the letters that had any import at all. They were mostly youthful blatherings that held very little credence as seen from my adult vantage point. But the thing was,

Otto saved them. Not for the letters but because I meant something to him. Just like all of those other correspondents meant to him. What he did with every reply to each of us and every saved missive was completely and entirely validate us. We mattered to him.

My ego, my vanity reading over those letters filled me with embarrassment. They sounded so young, so filled with such emotion—so many explanation points!!!!! But, my beloved brother Father John gently reminded me when I expressed such chagrin over them. He helped me see that I wrote the lion share of them from childhood into my teens and early twenties. So the adult in me should be a little more tolerant of the kid who penned those missives many years ago.

But all my high pitched pennings didn't seem to deter my darling Otto, nor Fritzi, who was helping him respond to all of us for years. This to me was a reflection of what validation looked like. It wasn't what we correspondents said most of the time, but rather the fact that we said it. And not only said it, but needed to say it to him in order to receive his guidance, his wisdom, his non-judgmental presence in our lives. Otto Frank listened to our hearts and validated each of us for simply being who we were.

The gift that Otto gave us was such a contrast to so much of what we're used to now-- critiquing or being critiqued in almost every situation with a discerning and oftentimes mean-spirited eye. No, our dear Otto Frank simply accepted us—rough edges, hyper drama and all.

The other top of the list validation moment for me back then featured Miep. When she and Bep discovered Anne's diary and notebooks strewn across the entire floor after the Nazis left them in disarray, she had a choice. She could have read them all as the other helpers so eagerly wanted to do, or she could have put them away unread. That was what she decided upon and that pivotal decision saved what would become "The Diary of Anne Frank". (Had she read one word of the writings she later explained she would have destroyed them since her name and that of all the other helpers were mentioned and in the process of being disguised, but Anne didn't have the time for name-changing.)

The reason Miep made that decision to gather all the writings unread was because she deeply respected Anne's need for privacy. Her love for the young girl who never shared a word of her writings and was emphatic about being guarded about their content was why Miep chose to honor her. She would wait until Anne returned from the camps and then hand them off to her at that time.

Even when Otto returned from the camps alone Miep still didn't reveal to him that she was holding Anne's cherished legacy in her desk. Miep was waiting to give them to Anne. Only when they learned that the young girl would never return from the Bergen-Belsen death camp is when Miep gave all of Anne's writings and diary to her bereaved father.

That was the epitome of validation. Her love and respect for Anne was Miep's priority and what would become an ultimate historic, transformative, literary masterpiece for generations upon generations to come.

From this moment on---and I know most of you already do this—save the gift you are given from one heart to yours—validating them as priceless, invaluable, something to be cherished for what it represents far more than what it is—a feather, a rock, a poem, a drawing, a shell, a letter, etc. I have all of these and far more gifted to me from so many and I treasure them more than words can say. They are the true validation of loving acceptance—echoes of the heart--in every way.

"Love is the absence of judgment." The Dalai Lama

"The Rock Within the Waves"

In 1944, when Otto Frank was in Auschwitz surrounded by the stench of death and dying, starvation, disease, and insurmountably unfathomable cruelty, he still held on. Focused on his beloved daughters and his identity as a father, that is what kept him alive. He told a young man next to him, to *"...call me 'Papa' for that is who I am."*

Longing to be reunited with his precious Anne and Margot, Otto kept that vision, that belief, that hope alive within him. No matter how heinous the world was around him, no one could destroy the core of his identity. He was still "Papa", and he would talk to this young man and they would discuss literature and music and all the beautiful aspects of life they remembered. Most of all he would think about Anne and Margot and being with them again as their father. That was who he was. That was his reason for being. And that was the very fuel that kept him alive until the moment of his liberation from the camp at the beginning of 1945. Barely standing, skeletal and sick, he lived to be with his children again. That passionate longing and belief saved his life.

The world famous psychiatrist Viktor Frankl, having been incarcerated in four different concentration camps between 1942-1945 learned that it is the pursuit of what humans personally find meaningful and hopeful that keeps them going. In his book, *Man's Search for Meaning*, time and time again Frankl proves that those who kept their sights on what mattered more than anything in their lives and never lost sight of that hope would inevitably survive the worst conditions in the world.

In my book, *Strength From Nature—Simple Lessons of Life Taught By the Most Unlikely Masters: The Nature Teachers*, I discuss the power of the rock within the pounding waves. We are the steadiness, the rock surrounded by the waves of life.

"If I am my own rock, then there is a stillness within me. There is peace. There is the ability to experience the waves of whatever my life is hit with, whatever washes over me, yet I don't lose myself in these waves. I remain. This doesn't mean I am impervious to life. I can feel the cold and the warmth and the joy and the sorrow and the ugly and the beautiful. But I am not any of those things, good or bad. I am simply who I am."

No matter how horrendous Otto's life had become, he never lost himself within the waves of his devastating sorrow. Ultimately, he made a choice to use his pain and loss to steady himself in the saving of his daughter's words and spirit. Papa Frank, the consummate father of Anne and Margot Frank, was the solid rock that emboldened the world and kept alive the legacy of his daughter's hopes and dreams and wishes to live on after her death.

So, I encourage you to always stay steady the course no matter how broken and rocky your path may be at present. Honor yourself, your sense of purpose, the strength within you that is very real and be that balance, that rock. Don't lose yourself in anything or anybody. Be the calm within the storm. That's how you will be able to get through whatever your challenges may happen to be.

"This is Me" (The Greatest Showman)
"I am brave, I am bruised
I am who I'm meant to be, this is me."
Songwriters: Justin Paul / Benj Pasek; This Is Me lyrics © Kobalt
Music Publishing Ltd.

"Be A Tree Of Hope"

At my most hopeless during the Sixties, Otto Frank encouraged me to plant a tree *"...even if the end of the world would be imminent."* And to punctuate the importance of life everlasting he had two trees planted in Israel in my name. I will never forget the impact such a gift had on me. It still reverberates today. Because trees are the literal and symbolic life breath of our planet. They are our lungs. The very air we breathe. If we lose them we all die and that's the truth.

Planting trees, a particularly beloved practical and symbolic act in the rabbinic imagination, embodies Jewish responsibility for each generation to cultivate resources for the next generation. Such deeply practical action within a spiritual framework is magnified by the dictum of Rabbi Yohanan ben Zakkai, *"If you have a sapling in your hand and are told, 'Look, the Messiah is here,' you should first plant the sapling and then go out to welcome the Messiah"* (The Fathers According to Rabbi Natan/ Avot de-Rabbi Natan, Version B 31).

So now I encourage you to figuratively as well as metaphorically please plant trees today. Our planet desperately needs replenishment after the devastation of wars, drought, floods, infestations, illegal logging—including the harvesting, transporting, processing, buying and selling of timber violating global national laws. The palm oil industry has devastated legions of wildlife and forests, as has the almost total destruction of the Amazon due to corporate greed.

Trees stretch to the sky with roots deep into the earth communicating to each other in myriad mystical ways we are only now realizing. They are both strong as well as malleable. They share food and infinite key survival information to each other and thrive best within their close knit communities. They are living, breathing, sensitive beings in far more ways than we ever knew. And they must be protected and cherished and honored no differently than all sentient beings. When we grow and flourish individually we grow and flourish together.

It is in our hands and hearts to each be trees of life; to plant renewal; to thrive as forests of hope for all living beings; to plant promise and belief in ourselves and in each other and within an eco-system that can and will heal even as the clock is ticking down. We mustn't ever give up hope.

www.onetreeplanted.org
"The clearest way into the Universe is through a forest wilderness."
-John Muir

"The Choice is in Your Hands"
"Just as ripples spread out when a single pebble is dropped into water, the actions of individuals can have far-reaching effects."
~ Dalai Lama

At the end of my talks to groups (before and after Covid!) I offer everyone to pick out a small smooth stone from a basket filled to the brim with pebbles in front of me. Eagerly they choose a little stone that resonates with them the most. And I explain to them the significance of such a small gift. That, I tell them, is a reminder of your choice. The moment we awaken until the moment we go to sleep we have choices as to how we want to look at, tackle, face, accept or not accept the life before us. The challenges. The joys. The sorrows. The surprises. The setbacks. The rewards. All of it. Life. How do we want to carry our burdens? The choice is always ours to make. To be positive or negative. We might need support to get us through our journeys, but there are always "Sherpas" – teachers, guides, healers, confidants, angels of all sorts to be there when we need them. They are there if we so choose to reach out to them for help.

But it is our choices in the end as to how and where and why we choose to see and experience each moment. We are the pebble, the smooth stone held in our hand and when dropped into a pool of water it is our ripple of energy—positive or negative—that effects others as it does our own selves.

Otto Frank made a choice to keep his daughter's legacy alive and help her words live on after death. That was her wish and because he chose to focus on that wish and her and all those killed in the Holocaust he became his own life-saver. He saved his life. He saved ours as well. Because of a choice not to let his pain decimate him; nor become bitter or revengeful. He moved forward and, choosing higher ground he uplifted us all, bringing us along with him.

Otto Frank chose love over hate. And we can do the same thing every moment of every day in our own lives. As you focus on the good over the evil; the happy over the sad; the healthy over the sick; the beauty over the ugliness; the hope over the hopelessness-- your ripple of effect will transform others in the same positive, loving ways as well. The choice is in your hands.

Fritzi and Otto in their backyard in Basel

Basel train station

Otto and Fritzi in Basel

Buddy Elias

Buddy and Gerti "Bambi" Elias

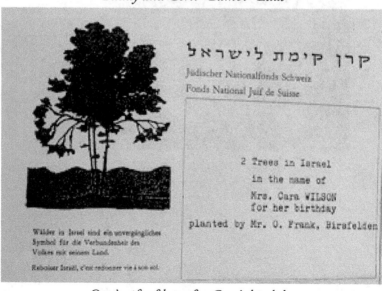

קרן קימת לישראל
Jüdischer Nationalfonds Schweiz
Fonds National Juif de Suisse

2 Trees in Israel
in the name of
Mrs. Cara WILSON
for her birthday
planted by Mr. O. Frank, Birsfelden

Wälder in Israel sind ein unvergängliches
Symbol für die Verbundenheit des
Volkes mit seinem Land.

Reboiser Israël, c'est redonner vie à son sol.

Otto's gift of hope for Cara's birthday

San Francisco gathering with Zvi, (Eva Schloss'
husband), Father John, Ryan Cooper, Cara and Eva

Buddy Elias standing before memorial grave of Anne and
Margot Frank in Bergen-Belsen.

Fritzi and Cara for Fritzi's birthday in London. Fritzi holding a tree- designed plate created by Cara for Fritzi.

Miep and Jan in Amsterdam

Jan, Father John, Miep in Cara's former home in Hollywood for Father John's ordination

Cara and Otto in Basel (Otto's backyard)

Otto at his writing desk

Otto at his writing desk

Fritzi, Cara, Otto in Basel

Jan, Miep and Cara in Cara's former home in Hollywood

Herbstgasse 11   Basel, 6.X.1959

Dear Cara,

　　　　　Thank you very much for your kind
letter in which you describe so nice your family life and tell me about your dear parents and
your sister. Well, I just want to say, that
it is quite normal, that sisters or brothers
quarrel together at times, and so did Margot
and Anne. I told them, that we were ~~three~~ brothers
and one sister and that we all are of very different character, that we quarreld a lot but - that
we always sticked together anyhow. We always
had a very close family-life and when we all
were grown-up, we helped one another whereever
possible.

　　　　　The main thing is to know, that you
intend the best, even if opinions differ. Your
sister is still very young and so are you. Life one
is not always gay and I hope that later-on~~e~~/will
be a support for the other in every difficulty
which may occur.

　　　　　You were so kind to send me a cheque
for the Foundation, which I turned over to Amsterdam. I thank you and your dear father for
it personally and in the name of the Foundation.
Every gift helps and is gratefully accepted.

　　　　　With best wishes to you and all the
members of your family I am with kind regards

June 7, 1960.

Otto Frank
Herbstgasse
Basle

Dear Cara,

I thank you very much for your kind
letter and I was very much surprised to receive
with it your lovely present. It was so sweet of
you to have made these cufflinks for me and I shall
always cherish your nice gift. I showed them to my
family and some friends and everybody admires the
skillful work. I wonder if you go to an a school
for applied art or if this kind of work is a hobby
of yours.

From all you write I can see that you were
interested in the Coronet article and the problems
concerning German youth. In fact I am interested in
youth all over the world and their problems. For
this purpose I stimulated the establishment of the
"International Youth Center of the Anne Frank
Foundation" in Amsterdam with the aim to foster understanding between young people and to work with
them in Anne's spirit against discrimination of all
kinds. As soon as we have English pamphlets, I shall
see to it that you get them.

Thanking you again, I am with kindest
regards and best wishes

Yours very sincerely

133

June 6, 1968

Dear Mr. Frank--

"America! America! God Shed His Light on Thee!" Today, Mr.
Frank, I don't know whether I can ever sing that song and
still believe in those words. I don't want to turn my back on
the land I've loved so fiercely, but the foundation, the "free"
soil beneath my feet is shaken. I'm frightened. And angry.
And ashamed. And terribly lost in the poisonous atmosphere of
fear...and hate. Bobby Kennedy is dead. Martin Luther King is
dead. John F. Kennedy is dead. Medger Evers is dead. All shot
by the bullets of mad men. Mad men who all some time in their
sad lives cried out to their neighbors for help...and no one heard...
or cared. Lonely men with scapegoats to vent their sick self-hate
upon.

Bobby Kennedy. A Saint? No. A Christ? No. No. No. A Man.
A man with youth and anger. A quick-silver mind and body. A
man not afraid of the mud or the darkness or the complexity of
the ghetto or the slick city. A man that Charles Evers, the
brother of the slain Medger Evers, believed in. The only white
man he really trusted. And his feelings were echoed by the majority
of the black people. Bobby Kennedy. A father and a husband and
a brother and a son and the only hope for peace in the minds of
millions all over the world.

134

Yes, the gentle, wise Senator Eugene McCarthy is a man I can
believe in as well. Robert Kennedy wanted to unite with this
man. He believed that together, their philosophies and their
followers would bring peace to our broken nation, to our broken
world. Where do I go now, Mr. Frank? Must I love and believe
in my world with the paranoid distrust and defense mechanism that
involves no real committment? To play it safe and not love...
because then I'll not be crushed. But then I won't have lived
totally...wholly...will I? When your world was destroyed...
how did you go about repairing it? How can I help strengthen
the world that is falling around me? I can't cradle my crying
nation to my breast and nurse it back to health. But I want to.
I can't storm the U.N. and shake each man by his shoulders and
beg him to tear down the walls. But I want to. I can't stand
in the middle of our land and scream for everyone to turn and
touch his neighbor's face...white hands on black cheek bones and
vice-versa...see the loneliness in each other's eyes...hear the
whisper before the scream...and the gunshot. But I want to. Will
we ever see into each other's eyes? The beautiful American Indians...
stony-faced and quiet in the silence of their neglected, unjust
worlds. And the Mexican-Americans..their vibrancy stifled by crowded
quarters...away from the big cities.

How can I bring a child into this world? What can I promise him?
Freedom? Peace? Love? Tolerance? Tomorrow? I don't mean to
be embittered. Or reject the substance, the core of living that
these great men died for in their fight for peace. Bobby Kennedy is
gone. And he was so briefly here. Just beginning to convince us of
a peaceful tomorrow.

And I was just beginning to break down my defenses. To extend
my hand to him. To be vulnerable in my love and respect for
him. Tuesday I voted for him. As did the majority of people here,
because he won the primary race in California. And then a mad man
decided he was too great for the world. As was the sick man's
molten hate too great to contain any longer. And he killed RFK.

Thank God Kent and I have each other during this mentally and
emotionally trying ordeal. We want to be strong. We don't
want to give up and forget what Bobby awakened within us. Kent
has helped me. When I start to strike out and hate the hate, he
reminds me of the power of love.

You are a forgiving man. A man of strength and inner battle-
scars. I could use some of your morale plasma right now.
I would like to help you, Mr. Frank, in the way you've helped me.
I would like to write a pamphlet or essay extending the philosphy
and love of Anne Frank. Your foundation is a great beginning. A
great attempt to reach the youth of the world and give them hope.
Today's youth needs hope. They need to believe in a tomorrow. A
beautiful tomorrow. A peaceful tomorrow. Not enough people know
about your foundation. Let me help you awaken their knowledge of
you and your work. Do you want this of me?

I feel a little better now, as do I always, once I've "talked" to
you. And as you also know, I love you. Please tell me what is
the date of your birth. I know it was some time in May, but you
never let me know when. I promise I won't embarrass you with a
huge Cecil B. DeMille production. I just want to know. Since

I'm already late, I wish you much health and happiness and a
happy, happy birthday and many, many more!!!!

Please, Mr. Frank, don't think I'm rejecting my America. I
love my country. My people. I just feel so helpless now.
At this moment, I can't see any shedding light. I feel so
empty. Along with your prayers, Mr. Frank, please include
America.

Until next time, be happy. Give my love and best wishes to
Mrs. Frank. My love to you. And I want to thank you for your
last letter, it was truly beautiful, as was your picture with
Mrs. Frank. I showed it to the family and they were just as
thrilled as I was. I'll send a recent picture of Kent and me
shortly. Kent sends his best wishes to you both as well.
He's been very busy with school and writing, but he plans on
writing you soon. He just won a scholarship from his department
for this summer. It entitles him to work for Screen Gems, a very
popular television production company out here. He will act as
an assistant to everybody on all the different shows. He'll get
to know who is who and they'll get to know him as well. Needless
to say, we're both quite excited. I'll be writing to you soon.
I hope I'll be in a happier, more optimistic frame of mind.
Thank you for listening, dear friend. God Bless You.

Much love,

Cara

Otto Frank
Buchenstr. 12
4127 Birsfelden
Tel. 41-48-08

June, 19, 1968.

ara,

          our last letter written under the impression
of the shock you felt after the assassination of
Robert Kennedy moved me very much. It was not a
letter,-it was a outcry. I understood you so well
as I share in many respects your feelings. I too,
as well as millions in the whole world are mourning over the death of R. Kennedy and thosewho before him became victims of fanatics. They all were excellent men on whom the hope of many good willing
people was set upon. If the murderers acted out
of personal grievances, one could not blame
"America" for these crimes. But one cannot help to
be suspicious that powerful, evil groups are working behind the screens. If this is really the
case and they can extend their power and succeed
in eliminating the progressive forces, I see the
future of America very gloomily.

          If nothing will be done to end the Vietnam
war and to help the poor and neglected masses,
there really is the danger of an uprising, a civil
war. The pathetic words of Rev. Abernathy addressing the crowds at the march of the poor, that this
is the last chance of a peaceful solution, makes
one shudder.

          But there is still an alternative. IHXYHHFX
AdHHHFHIHXHYHHH There are millions who are feeling their responsibilities just as you do.

          In your democratic system there is the possi-
bility of influencing affairs by election. Much wil
depend on the next President and his advisers. As
far as we can judge from here however, not one of
the candidates can replace Kennedy. Though McCarthy
has about the same aims, he seems not to have the
brilliant, energetic personality, but one must
hope that he will grow with his duties, should he

be elected. Or should the republican party be
given a chance with Rockefeller?

Though the situation is far from satisfactory, you must not desperate. Never give up!

I remember to have once read a sentence: "If
the end of the world would be imminent, I still
would plant a tree to-day." When we lived in the
secret annexe we had the device " "Fac et spera"
which means :"Work and hope". I do not know, if I
ever wrote this to you.

So you should not ask if you should bring a
child into this world. Life goes on and perhaps
your child will bring the world one step further.
Anne who died as a victim of injustice and hatred,
achieved something for mankind in her short life.
Perhaps the new generation will live under quite
different circumstances than we can imagine now
and will have a quite different feeling of happiness.

You are right that at certain periods of my
existence the world around me collapsed. When most
of the people of my country, Germany turned into
hordes of nationalistic, cruel antisemitic criminals, I had to face the consequences and though
this did hurt me deeply I realized that Germany
was not the world and I left for ever.

When I returned from concentration-camp alone,
I saw that a tragedy of unexpressible extent had
hit the Jews, my people, and I was spared as one of
them to testify, one of those who had lost his dear
ones

It was not in my nature to sit down and mourn.
I had good people around me and Anne's Diary
helped me a great deal to gain again a positive
outlook on life. I hoped by publishing it to help
many people in the same way and this turned out
to be true.

When later the Anne Frank Foundation was
established I wanted it to work in the spirit of
Anne's ideals for peace and understanding among
peoples.

But as you can imagine we are working on a rather
small scale as we only can reach and try to influence people who are coming to the Anne Frank
House. It was always my wish to make the center
of an international organisation with branches in
many countries, which would have to deal with
their specific problems. Up to now this was not
possible.

Your are asking me what you could do to sp
spread the hope which is contained in Anne's Diary to the benefit of the youth of your country.
May be that through a pamphlet, as you propose it
an action could be started and an Anne Frank
group formed. This group should issue a paper in
which young people could express themselves freely, trying to find positive answers to the many-
fold problems which divide America. F.i.U.S.A.
has the sad reputaion to have the highest rate
of crime and dope in the world. Why not fight
against the horror-and crime films and literature?
I know that big business would oppose the oppression of such films. Ammunition and war-material
industries are against the limiting of the sale
of weapons. Only youth with ideals could take a
stand against these evils. This is just one idea.

But how could such a paper be financed and
distributed? I am thinking of subscription and
many volontary helpers.

Two years ago a lady Mrs. M.Myers attended
our Int. Youth Conference in Amsterdam. She got
very enthousastic about the Foundation and its
work and from this time on, she is writing to
me asking what she could do to help. Her address
is: 507 South Madison Ave. Apt. 3, Pasadena, Cal.
91106. Her husband has a printing firm.

Perhaps you would like to contact her and
if some sort of a plan could be worked out, I
could give you more names of people in California
who may want to be of assistance.

I am so glad that you have Kent at your
side in these difficult times. He gives you sx
strength and comfort. The harmony between you
should enable you to cope with every situation.

Dearest Cara,
Now my darling Otto has left me and all his friends in the world. Though I know that he wanted to die after his long and fulfilled life with the many sad but also happy events I shall miss him terribly. — I am glad however that you still saw him when he was his own lovable self. — Luckily he did not suffer and passed away peacefully.
I received your interesting article. You really did spend a wonderful job. When and where will it be published? I hope it will help you on your way to become a journalist or a writer.
I am now with my daughter and her family but all are surrounding me with their love. But soon I shall go home to start my life alone after 28 happy years. Lots of love to the 4 of you. affectionately yours,
Fritzi

September 19 80.

I would like to thank you sincerely for the friendship and heart-felt sympathy shown to me at the occasion of the passing-away of my beloved, unforgetable husband, Otto Frank.

Appendix

The Diary of a Young Girl, by Anne Frank. The definitive edition, with new translaton edited by Otto Frank and Mirjam Pressler, translated by Susan Massotty, (Doubleday.)

The Diary of Anne Frank, The Critical Edition, prepared by the Netherlands State Institute for War Documentation, Introduced by Harry Paape, Gerrold van der Stroom and David Barnouw, with a summary of the report by the State Forensic Science Laboratory of the Ministry of Justice compiled by H.J.J. Hardy, Edited by David Barnouw and Gerrold van der Stroom, (Translated by Arnold J. Pomerans and B.M. Mooyaart-Doubleday.)

Anne Frank – The Book, The Life, The Afterlife, by Francine Prose, Harper (a division of HarperCollins Publishers).

Anne Frank—Beyond the Diary. A Photographic Remembrance, by Ruud van der Rol and Rian Verhoeven, for the Anne Frank House, translated by Tony Langham and Plym Peters. Introduction by Anna Quindlen (Viking, published by the Penguin Group.)

The Last Seven Months of Anne Frank, Willy Lindwer. Translated from the Dutch by Alison Meersschaert. New York: Anchor Books (a division of Random House, Inc.).

Eva's Story (A Survivor's Tale by the Step-Sister of Anne Frank), Eva Schloss with Evelyn Julia Kent; (W H Allen, London.)

After Auschwitz: A story of heartbreak and survival by the stepsister of Anne Frank, by Eva Schloss

The Promise: A Moving Story of a Family in the Holocaust, Commentary by Barbara Powers, co-author with Eva Schloss, (London, Penguin Books.)

The Hidden Life of Otto Frank, by Carol Ann Lee, (Harper Perennial.)

Roses From The Earth, The Biography of Anne Frank, by Carol Anne Lee, (Penguin Books.)

Anne Frank Remembered—The Story of the Woman Who Helped to Hide the Frank Family. By Miep Gies with Alison Leslie Gold. (A Touchstone book, published by Simon & Schuster.)

Anne Frank's Family, by Mirjam Pressler, chronicled by Gerti Elias, wife of Buddy Elias, nephew of Otto Frank, first cousin of Anne Frank, (Random House, Inc.)

The Last Seven Months of Anne Frank, by Wally Lindwer. (An Achor book, published by Doubleday.)

We Never Said Goodbye – Memories of Otto Frank, by Ryan M. Cooper

For the Sake of the Children: The Letters Between Otto Frank and Nathan Straus, Jr., by Joan Adler (author and publisher), Executive Director of the Straus Historical Society, Post Office Box 416, Smithtown, NY 11787-0416, 631-724-4487 info@straushistory.org www.straushistoricalsociety.org

"Meeting" Anne Frank: An Anthology, by Tim Whittome , with Forward by Joop Van Wijk-Voskuijl

Anne Frank, The Untold Story. The Hidden Truth About Elli Vossen, the Youngest Helper of the Secret Annex, by Joop Van Wijk-Voskuijl and Jeroen De Bruyn www.annefrank-theuntoldstory.com
ISBN: 978-90-829013-0-6

Beautiful books about Anne Frank in Italian:
" Quando dal cielo cadevano le stelle" by Federica Pannocchia (Eden Editori, 2016)

"Siamo chi eravamo" by Federica Pannocchia (Porto Seguro Editore, 2021)

CHARITABLE FOUNDATIONS

The Anne Frank-Fonds Foundation
Steinengraben 18, 4051 Basel, Switzerland
- Initiated and financed by the ANNE FRANK Shoah Library at the German library in Leipzig, Germany.
- Supports Israeli-Palestinian peace organizations.
- Co-finances exchange visits and meetings among young Germans, Israelis, and Arabs.
- Supports other charitable activities that seek to combat all forms of racism and anti-Semitism.

Anne Frank House, now a museum supporting extensive public activities against all forms of discrimination:

Anne Frank Stichting
Westermarkt 10
Postbus 730
1000 AS Amsterdam, the Netherlands
www.annefrank.org
US dial: 011-31-20-556-7100
Fax #: 011-31-20-620-7999

Anne Frank House
Museum visitors address:
Westermarkt 20
1016 DK Amsterdam
Prinsengracht 263
Amsterdam
tel +31 20 556 71 05

Anne Frank Center For Mutual Respect, U.S.A.
44 Park Place
New York, NY 10007
212-431-7993
www.annefrank.com

United States Holocaust Memorial Museum
100 Raoul Wallenberg Place, SW
Washington, DC 20024-2126
www.ushmm.org

Cara Wilson-Granat

Storyteller/Author/TEDx Speaker, Cara Wilson-Granat captivates readers and international audiences with the telling of the Anne Frank story and the ensuing passion and shared lessons of Otto Frank to keep his daughter's legacy alive. Guided by the wisdom and strength of Otto's words, Cara helps her audiences explore the lessons of history—lessons which, sadly, the world continues to revisit in violent and painful ways today. Featuring the long correspondence between Cara and Otto Frank against the backdrop of the turbulent Sixties and more, we are invited into their personal and loving friendship—part of a far-reaching global audience of youth Otto Frank also inspired.

Cara, who lives in Colorado with her husband, Peter and cat Boo, is also the author of ***Strength from Nature—Simple Lessons of Life Taught By the Most Unlikely Masters: The Nature Teachers.*** Cara also co-wrote, with Mary Kate Scandone, ***Nick of Time—The Nick Scandone Story: A Champion Paralympian Turns a Death Sentence Into Gold.***

www.wordsfromcara.com
cara@wordsfromcara.com

CPSIA information can be obtained
at www.ICGtesting.com
Printed in the USA
BVHW040447081221
623485BV00003B/8